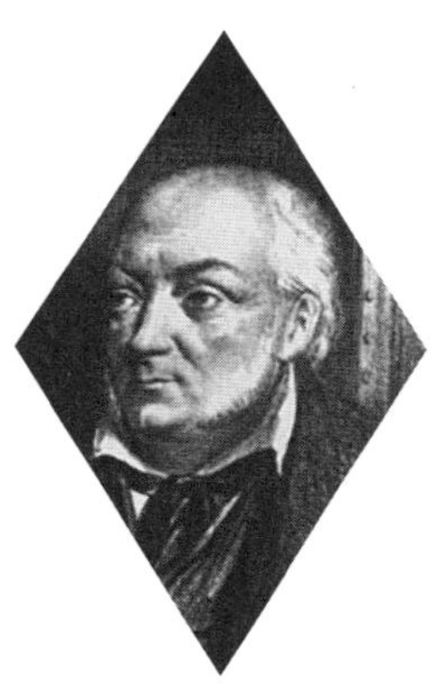

EVERYTHING IS IN EVERYTHING

JACQUES RANCIÈRE *Between* INTELLECTUAL EMANCIPATION *and* AESTHETIC EDUCATION

Edited by
JASON E. SMITH & ANNETTE WEISSER

Art Center Graduate Press

The essays collected in this volume represent versions of papers presented at the "Everything is in Everything: From Intellectual Emancipation to Aesthetic Education" symposium hosted by the Graduate Studies in Art program at Art Center College of Design on March 11-12, 2011. The lone exception is the interview that Jacques Rancière, not being able to attend this conference, has allowed us to translate and publish here.

Of the many people who contributed to the staging of the conference and the publication of this volume, the editors would like to single out Art Center's President, Lorne Buchman, and its Provost, Fred Fehlau, for their unflagging encouragement and support in making this event and the resulting publication possible. The Chair of the Graduate Studies in Art program, Jeremy Gilbert-Rolfe, was enthusiastic about the conference and instrumental at every step of the way in seeing it, and this publication, into reality. Finally, we would like to thank our students in the Graduate Studies in Art program, and in particular the group of students who participated in our two-semester reading group on Jacques Rancière's work, for their energy, insight, and interest in the questions addressed in this volume.

The Editors

PREFACE

Jeremy Gilbert-Rolfe

Our conference began with our keynote speaker being moved to our building's roof because of the oversized crowd on what unfortunately turned out to be an unusually cold night in Southern California, and I took it as a good sign that no one left, choosing instead to shiver not so much appreciatively as involuntarily. I am pleased to be able to say that after that things got even better. By the end of the following day signs of intense disagreement between people who fundamentally agreed were visible everywhere. In my view, that is an indication that something was done by way of producing useful discourse.

It was very important to us that we were able to do this conference, which we hope will be the first of an ongoing series which will take place every two years, because it is important to us to have an active relationship with the world beyond and around our central concern with making art.[1] We started the Graduate Art Program in 1986 and from the beginning have tried to be a program in which artists are exposed to theory in a helpful way that is integrated with the work they do in the studio. At orientation I always tell the new candidates that we want to be a program from which our graduates leave feeling as comfortable with French philosophy as with American art dealers and, thinking that the way to achieve this is to have minimum contact with the latter and maximum contact with the former while in school, we have managed quite a good history with French intellectuals. In the last five years, Alain Badiou has spoken here more than once, as has Slavoj Zizek, and in past decades we held a sort of conference in a casino on the Nevada border with Jean Baudrillard, and Félix Guattari gave what may have been one of his last lectures here. But we felt this conference went beyond reminding people that we are a graduate program that was open to theory and where theory as well as practice take place—or where they are inseparable in practice. We thought it was specifically important, because that is what we try to do in our program, to have a conference in which artists and theorists sat on panels together, instead, as Annette Weisser put it, of the theorists talking and the artists doing things during the breaks. In our Program artists and theorists teach together in the same room and our candidates engage equally with both and the conference reflected that approach. In a related regard it was of course similarly useful to us all that the conference was genuinely international in its composition, content, and scope.

It was also particularly important to us because it was about Rancière. His insistence on the irreversible importance of the aesthetic is of crucial importance to what goes on in our school. Our faculty is diverse, so here I'll put forward what is my own view. That is that Rancière provides a way into two dilemmas in contemporary art, one having to do with how much of it amounts to the suppression of the aesthetic in the name of the political, the other with another kind of historical problem. There are quite a lot of people who would not agree with my feeling that most art nowadays is anthropological rather than aesthetic in origin and intent, or would at least reject such a description of the distinction I discern. And as the contents of the present volume attest, the question of where the aesthetic is being located and what it's being allowed to do to and with the political tends to be presented in reverse or at least modified form, as a question of what the political may do if it uses the aesthetic as a negative example of how to think.

That is in my view an historical problem in the sense of being a problem that derives from where art's general episteme has been recently. It matters little whether the question be approached from one direction or the other, and if this conference did nothing else it will have brought home to its audience the proximity of a certain defining characteristic of both art and politics, which is that both require a working theory of action as a necessity. Before they can be either art or politics, they must be practices after but also before they are ideas. This I think is variously evident in the papers reprinted here, and is in my view inherent in Rancière's position on categories and competence, when he speaks of "a 'primary aesthetics' in the sense that even practices that are not 'artistic' such as politics presuppose the sensible configuration of a certain world: politics defines a common world, it defines objects as common, which is also to say that it also excludes certain objects from this community. It also defines the form of competence required to see these common objects, to discuss them and to act with regard to them: that is, it distinguishes between those who have this competence and those who do not."[2]

That also relates to the other kind of historical problem I mentioned, for which I personally look for answers anywhere the aesthetic is still permitted to exist, and which will I think be recognizable to all when presented in the following terms. It is still the case that some part of art education takes place between now quite elderly artists who worked their way through modernism to their present condition, and younger colleagues and particularly students who were born just after it. Soon the elderly ones will be gone and there will only be different states of the post-modern talking to one another in art schools. Rancière's contribution to thinking about the post-modern as something other than the not-modern, as part of the question of politics and its relation to the historical condition of Schiller's idea that the origin of the aesthetic object is not in nature but in the aesthetic object, will I think keep him somewhere near the center of pedagogy in graduate art education for the foreseeable future. I think that what was done here was and will be useful in that regard to both artists and scholars, and should like to end this brief preface to their work by personally thanking the participants whose papers are presented here for letting us publish them.

1 We are tentatively proposing a conference on how art got from about 1970 to here for 2013; and on the differences between art and design that may be exposed through a genealogical reading of both terms, and thence be the basis for a better theory of what they might have in common, for the year 2015.

2 See the interview with Rancière published in this volume, pp. 10–38.

1

A POLITICS OF AESTHETIC INDETERMINATION: AN INTERVIEW WITH FRANK RUDA & JAN VOELKER

Jacques Rancière

In *The Distribution of the Sensible,* you spoke of a "primary aesthetics" on the basis of which it is possible to grasp the aesthetic regime of art.[1] Can you explain these two concepts? Is there a distance between the two? Or rather, how can the relationship between the distribution of the sensible and the aesthetic regime be described? And, to ask still one more question, how does the specific idea of the aesthetic regime relate to the idea of distribution?

Jacques Rancière: I spoke of a "primary aesthetics" in the sense that even practices that are not "artistic," such as politics, presuppose the sensible configuration of a certain world: politics defines a common world, it defines objects as common, which is also to say that it excludes certain objects from this community. And politics defines the form of competence required to see these common objects, to discuss them and to act with regard to them: that is, it distinguishes between those who have this competence and those who do not. Now, this distinction is a matter of sensible evidence or obviousness before being a matter of philosophical or juridical definition. Aristotle defines political capacity on the basis of the possession of a human language that can discuss and debate, as opposed to the voice of the animal that expresses mere pleasure and pain. All it takes to relegate the vast majority of humanity outside of the political is to not "see" that they speak, to reduce their speech to the mere noise of animal life. The political is therefore first of all the debate over what is given sensibly, on what is seen, on the way what is seen is sayable and over who can see and say it. This brings into play, then, a distribution of the visible, the sayable and the doable, in both senses of the word *partage*[2]: what is made common, but also what draws the line between and separates the two sides of what is seeable and invisible, audible and inaudible, possible and impossible, and therefore also "divides" those who speak from those who do not, those who can from those who cannot, etc. This primary distribution is what I have called the distribution of the sensible, or the distribution of the forms that structure common experience. We could speak of a priori forms of common, sensible experience if we transpose and expand Kant's concept. But these a priori forms are always historically determined forms, and this does not simply mean forms that exist in such and such an historical period. For these forms themselves define certain types of historicity: various senses of history, delimitations of what is or is not historical, distinguishing between those who "make" history and those who do not. And these forms are above all polemical forms. They are the product of tensions and conflicts: the history of politics is the history of the ways those who were not "seen" to be capable of discerning and judging common affairs have been able to redraw the field of the visible, the sayable and the thinkable that shuts them up within this incapacity. A distribution of the sensible is always an affair of force.

It is within this historical and polemical framework that the regimes of identifications of the arts are defined, as the regimes of perception and thought that separate out certain activities recognized as arts, fine arts, or art. These divisions are always ways of deciding between multiple activities that put to work a certain art (i.e. a certain know-how) and assign them to a certain sensible milieu. They always define, therefore, a certain form of the distribution of the sensible. I therefore proposed to call that regime where activities that we call arts are not autonomized as such but are immediately assimilated to the ways of being of a community, the ethical regime: for this regime, dance is a ritual or a therapy, poetry a form of education, the theater a civic festival, etc. I have proposed that we call poetic or representative that regime where mimetic activities are defined by their own, proper sensible sphere: these activities are thought of as technical inventions producing specific forms of affection, such as fear and pity in tragedy. This regime presupposes an agreement between the rules for producing the arts (*poesis*) and the laws of human sensibility (*aisthesis*). But this human sensibility is in fact clearly marked by an entire system of analogies with social hierarchies: there are, in this regime, representable things and things that are not representable, noble forms appropriate to great subjects, inferior forms suitable to low subjects, a hierarchy of arts and genres. I call, finally, the aesthetic regime the regime of art that no longer presupposes any form of adequation or any form of hierarchy of this type. This regime qualifies things as art not according to the rules of their production but by their belonging to a sensorium of their own and to a specific mode of experience. This does not mean we are in a world of pure spirits with no relation to social realities. This means that the products of the arts are no longer determined by the degree of elevation of the subjects they treat, the functions they carry out or the social powers they serve. They inscribe themselves in a sphere of experience proper to them. It is only in this regime that Art exists as such, rather than the arts or fine arts, and that it has a history (which can be distinguished from the "lives of famous artists") and institutions that are proper to it: the museum, for example, where a statue of a Greek god, a representation of a crucifixion, a royal portrait and a Flemish tavern scene all engage the same gaze, one that is indifferent to the original destination of the works and the relative elevation of their subject; or the concert hall where music is simply given as music, with no relation to a text or a function. There is no longer any relation between artistic normativity and a hierarchical distribution of the sensible. This does not mean that art defines itself solely "by itself." For it is precisely this "itself" that poses a problem: what is "proper" to art is a sphere of experience, and not the laws or properties of its objects. On one hand, there are no longer any noble or low subjects, noble or vulgar genres, since anything can enter the realm of art: the representation of a tavern scene or the adulterous tales of a peasant's daughter belong to art just as much as princely loves and splendor. But above all, there is no longer any correspondence between *poesis* and *aisthesis*: no more rules allowing us to say why things are beautiful or not, no more presupposition of a correspondence between the rules of art and the laws of sensibility. When Kant defines the beautiful on the basis of the free, non-hierarchical relation between the intellectual and sensible faculties, when he distinguishes the object of aesthetic judgment from that of knowledge or desire, he emphasizes this double suspension of both the hierarchy of knowledge and the hierarchy of goods and sizes. This is what Schiller radicalizes: aesthetic experience ruins the hierarchies that submit matter to form, sensibility to intelligence, and passivity to activity. It ruins the distribution of the sensible that legitimates domination by distinguishing between men with educated senses and those with crude ones. And this is what allows the aesthetic regime to conceptualize a freedom and an equality that are sensible realities and not simply legal and governmental formulas. It is to this conception that we see grafted the dream of an aesthetic revolution that would realize in the very forms of lived experience a freedom and an equality otherwise condemned to remain, in their simply political form, abstract. It is not a matter of an idealist utopia: the aesthetic regime of art gives a new distribution of the sensible as condition of possibility for aesthetic experience. It includes, in the very constitution of this experience, a political dimension.

In *The Distribution of the Sensible* you have written that this distribution defines all that is given to sensible experience in general. The aesthetic regime of art identifies, if we can put it this way, works of art that can sound out and even change this space of possible sensibility. How far should this distribution be thought to extend? Does it concern not simply the seeable and the sayable, but the audible, the affective, the olfactory as well?

JR: We must distinguish the sensible from the sensory. The sensory would be defined as the pure information or the pure stimulus produced by a sense. The sensible is sense distributed: the senses related to sense, the visible articulated with the sayable, the interpreted, evaluated, etc. Different distributions of the sensible do not modify our perception of colors as sensual information. But color is precisely always more than colors. Color is inscribed in a distribution of the sensible that relates it to something other than itself: line, or drawing. In the ethical regime, color is often associated with a symbolic value. In the representative regime, it is situated in a hierarchical relation of subordination to drawing. The aesthetic regime disrupts this subordination of colored matter to drawn form. Doing so, it modifies the sensible perception of color itself. When the criticism of the nineteenth century looks at painting, color ceases being a property of the represented subject or an ornament spread out over the represented body. It tends to become a reality in itself, an event of matter. It has value in itself, which also means that the matter of judging it in fact no longer belongs only to connoisseurs alone, it belongs to all. Color, in this way, is inscribed in a distribution of the sensible that is also a distribution of competences. You could say the same thing for sound. The distribution of the sensible does not alter the frequency and intensity of sonorous signals. It alters, instead, the inscription of sonorous sequences in a world of experience. A concept such as music is remarkable from this perspective: it introduces a differentiation into the domain of sounds. Now, this differentiation puts into play categories that are exterior to the domain of sound: "music" means "what depends on the muses." What depends on the muses involves another order than that of simple technical capacity: the law that separates elite pleasures from artisanal know-how and vulgar pleasures. "Music" introduces, therefore, a social distribution into the universe of sounds. And social hierarchy presents itself, for its part, first of all as a matter of sensorial difference. People of taste, Voltaire says, do not have the same senses as vulgar people. This does not mean that they do not perceive the same sonorous intensities. But it does mean that people of taste live in a world normed by music while the others live in a world normed by noise. The aesthetic regime puts into question this sensible distribution of two humanities, the distribution between the world of noise and the world of music. But it does so by also emancipating musical "noise" from the different functions music was associated with: religious ceremony, the accompaniment of words in theater, entertainment at meetings of high society, etc. This is the sense of the emancipation of instrumental practice at the end of the eighteenth century: a music that illustrates nothing, that serves no function. This sensible revolution is different, for me, than the sensorial revolution that certain artists dreamed of at the end of the nineteenth century and the middle of the twentieth: Rimbaud's poetry, which would be accessible to all the senses, the synaesthetic ambitions of the symbolist era, Antonin Artaud's theater of cruelty, etc. In these cases, what was at stake was, properly speaking, the defining of another sensoriality altogether. There is, in the same way, an assimilation of the sensible to the sensory when Adorno declares that certain musical chords can no longer be heard. For me, these declarations of a properly sensorial rupture are only particular ways of interpreting the aesthetic revolution and the new distribution of the sensible it lays out.

One of the most important references you use in order to set out the stakes of the aesthetic regime is Schiller. What is, for you, the historically specific significance of Schiller? Perhaps we can take as an example a notion that is central for this regime: the signification of life. In the *15th Letter on Aesthetic Education*, to which you often refer, Schiller calls life an object of the sense-drive, while *Gestalt* or form is deemed the object of the form-drive. On many occasions you have remarked that the Art of the aesthetic regime becomes Life. Put another way, we might say that it adapts itself to the auto-poesis of life. How would you describe the role of life in the aesthetic regime?

JR: With the concept of "life" you can understand very different, even opposed things: life is the deployment of a power, whether biological, historical, or ontological, but it is also, inversely, ordinary life, in opposition to the exceptional character of political action, the work of art, etc. To speak in terms of the distribution of the sensible is to consider a certain knotting together, a certain distribution of these different "lives." For example, the Aristotelian paradigm of the dramatic poem claims for itself one life—that of the organic body with its functional and harmoniously distributed members—while rejecting another: life as a simple succession of events, as opposed to tragedy and its constructed linkage of events. It is clear that this valorization of life as the form of the poem and the devalorization of life at the level of content is a translation of the hierarchy between two sorts of lives: the life of those who act and the life of those who merely live. "Life," then, describes a certain symbolic physiology of the social body. It is this physiology that Schiller disturbs by introducing a new vital power, a third drive [*Trieb*]. Insofar as you understand life as an object of the sense-drive, you remain within the active/passive hierarchy. With the play-drive, you are dealing with a vital power that disorders this distribution of lives. It is a new configuration of the relation between life and artistic forms that define it. This configuration institutes a separate sphere of life for aesthetic experience (since play takes leave of the opposition between the intellectual and the sensible) but revokes in its turn any distinction between the artistic productions and the products of others spheres of experience (since there is no hierarchy of lives that commands the content of art). On the one hand, artistic experience sets out to define a specific form of experience, separate from other forms. In this sense, it is opposed to a certain "life," that is, to a hierarchical distribution of the sensible where the arts are destined to serve or to illustrate worldly or spiritual greatness (religion, monarchy, aristocratic life) and where the fine arts that are devoted to the greatness and to the leisure of noble life are separated from the mechanical arts bound to the necessities of life. This unbinding of art from traditional hierarchical functions corresponds to the revocation of the internal hierarchy through which artistic practice defines itself: the imposition of intelligent, active form on a passive, sensible materiality. The Kantian conception of judgments of taste and the Schillerian conceptualization of the "play-drive" [*Spieltrieb*] are organized around the refutation of this distribution of the active and passive. But this divorce between art and a certain life also means that there are no longer any properly artistic subjects, there is no longer any border between what belongs to the dignity of the fine arts and what belongs to ordinary experience. The representative tradition transformed mimesis into the construction of linked "systems of actions" and opposed this distribution of actions to the "story" that is simply the reproduction of life, that is, of the conditions of beings excluded from the domain of action and therefore condemned to the simple reproduction of existence. From now on, the border between action and life no longer has any consistency. Anything can enter into art. And, in parallel fashion, there is no longer any separation between a refined and an uncouth nature: art no longer has specific producers nor privileged addressees. This double revocation has nourished the idea of an art become similar to life. An art that would have been, in the past, that of Phidias and Socrates; an art similar to the deployment of the life of a collectivity; an art that in the future is called upon to be one with the production of new forms of life. "Life" should be understood here in the sense of a determined distribution of the sensible rather than in a biological or ontological sense.

Would you say that there is a relation between the aesthetic regime of art and the science of life that was just emerging at the same historical moment?

JR: It is not the emergence of life as a scientific concept that intervenes all alone in this case. Let's simply say that this emergence defines a power of immanence and a form of universality that is part of the refutation of hierarchies between mind and body, or form and matter. But "life" is not only the concept of what unites the living, it is also the field of differentiation in which the "simply biological," "naked life," defines an inferior "way of life": it is this distribution that is put into question by both the political revolution and the aesthetic revolution. The new science of life is not enough on its own to suppress it, even if it plays a part.

When you speak of the aesthetic regime, how do you understand the relation between the concepts of beauty, equality and truth? And what does each term mean in the aesthetic regime of art?

JR: Let's begin with the relation between beauty and equality. The principle of the aesthetic regime is first of all that beauty is indifferent to the quality of the subject. The display of fruits or fish, the sentiments of a simple being, an adulteress in a small provincial town, are just as likely to be beautiful as an image of the Olympian gods or the representation of the dashing acts of princes. This means as well that the new principle of the beautiful is a principle of neutralization: the little beggar boys painted by Murillo have the insouciance of Olympian gods, Hegel says. It is clear, then, that the equality of the street children with the Olympians is tied to another equality: that which neutralizes, on the body, the expression of actions, sentiments, and thoughts. Aesthetic equality is first of all the neutralization of a certain regime of expressivity. The little beggar boys are as beautiful as the Belvedere Torso celebrated by Winckelmann. They are beautiful because, like the Torso, they say and do nothing, because their bodies express nothing. What this new beauty annuls is the system by which bodies present signs that translate thoughts or sentiments, summarize actions, etc. What it annuls, then, is the system of verisimilitude [*vraisemblance*]. Now, verisimilitude is the way the representative regime holds the truth at a distance. Aristotle's mimesis was opposed to Plato's: the works of poets were not to be judged to be deceptive images or as morally dubious models. They have to be judged from the point of view of their coherence alone, from the coherence of the groups of actions, the forms and signs they deploy (which were no less bound, of course, to external norms and hierarchies). It is this coherence that the aesthetic regime comes to ruin by declaring all subjects to be indifferent and by revoking the classical models with their construction of actions and their expression of passions. Beauty no longer finds its norm in verisimilitude. It is once again related to truth. But this truth has no criteria. It must impose itself by its own power, it must be *index sui*. But this self-demonstration occurs, paradoxically, through a self-alteration, through a self-difference. We find this paradox at the heart of all the relatively strong affirmations of the question of truth in the aesthetic regime. It is the sexual division of tasks between the poem and music that sustains the Wagnerian will to the total work of art. It is Dionysian truth's need for the Apollonian veil that is at the heart of Nietzsche's definition of tragedy. We find the same paradox in Flaubert's reflection on literature: there are no longer any subjects, the work rests on itself alone, it makes itself its own proof, sentence by sentence. But the truth or the falsity of the sentence is something that is known only through its sonority. Proust resolves this problem in a completely different way, by doubling the truth of the book: on the one hand, the truth is revealed as the conclusion of an apprenticeship knowingly constructed by the author as a traversal of anti-artistic errors; on the other hand, the truth appears in the form of the pure event that surprises and overtakes the subject and writes itself in him without him knowing it.

Would you say that the art of our time is always subject to the rules of the aesthetic regime? How can we distinguish a video installation from the works of Schiller? What do they have in common, and what separates them? This question points, to be sure, toward the idea of postmodernity. For you, the concepts of modernity and postmodernity are useless. But how would you describe the tendencies of contemporary art, particularly those that tend toward a desubjectivation through the use of media and computers?

JR: We should first of all make clear that the aesthetic regime is neither Schiller's invention nor is it the invention of any writer or philosopher, even if certain of them conceptualized some of its basic elements. Let's also make clear that this regime is defined not by rules but by a disordering [*dérèglement*]. First, in the sense that anything can become the subject of art, and then in the sense that this regime abolishes the system of Fine Arts, which defines several things at once: the separation between the mechanical and liberal arts, the determination of what is proper to each art, and the forms of correspondence among them. It is because the aesthetic regime blurred the borders between what is art and what is mechanical, between what is poetic and what is prosaic, that the "mechanical" arts (photography, cinema, video) have been able to assume a place in art. We must therefore cast doubt on the idea that new technologies have the power to introduce breaks in the paradigms of art. If you take video and its derived forms, you will notice that its apparatus lends itself to any number of possible identifications. In the 1970s, militant American artists willingly considered it to be a simple technology used to accompany and diffuse their performances, and therefore serving the same cause they did: the demystification of great art. In the 1980s, there was an attempt by artists such as Gary Hill, Woody and Steina Vasulka or Thierry Kuntzel to define video as an art whose specific means give it a specific experimental role. This was what one might call the "modernist" age of video.

But things very quickly got blurry. In these same years, Godard used the technical means of video to compose, in *Histoire(s) du Cinéma*, an imaginary museum of cinema. Today, video is a medium that lends itself to very different uses, from the "chamber dramas" of artists like Eija-Liisa Ahtila to Bill Viola's Giotto fresco cycles. It participates in this blurring of distinctions among arts that characterizes the entire aesthetic regime of art and not merely the small episode called "postmodernism." This blurring also includes new technologies. The so-called postmodern discourse often only layers a varnish of cynical denial over the old complaint that the coldness of machines kills the warmth of love, the color of flowers or the shining of the stars. But subjectivity is not lost with apparatuses. A page of text is no less subjective on a screen than it is on a sheet of paper; a photographic shot is no less subjective if it is digital rather than analogue. In music, synthesizers and computers lent themselves both to serial rigor and to all the musical eclecticisms that followed. Digitization suppresses nothing of the subjectivity of the gaze or of affect. It is only in the name of a superficial discourse on contemporary "anaesthesia," the triumph of the "spectacle," of the media, etc., that you can oppose technological apparatuses to sensible subjectivity. Many contemporary films, such as Wong Kar-Wai's *Three Times* or Eric Khoo's *Be with Me* have shown that you can put a whole drama on the screen of a mobile telephone: in *Be with Me*, for instance, the hand that presses "delete" after each incoming "i love u."

In any case, my problem is not that of proposing frameworks that envelop everything. It is to put into question a certain number of categorical distributions whose explanatory value is extremely weak but that have nevertheless imposed themselves due to a certain spirit of the times. The declaration of the "postmodern" is, for the most part: we no longer believe in the revolutionary potential of art or anything else for that matter. With this, you are not really equipped to analyze the cinema, video or music of today, no more than you were equipped to analyze the painting of Manet, Kandinsky or Malevich with modernist categories.

What can a painting, a sculpture, a novel or a film offer us today? And what can a painting that is 30,000 years old mean for us today?

JR: To think the compossibility of these two emotions is to think the power of indetermination that is at the heart of the aesthetic affect. A prehistoric painting is a painting that we can appreciate in multiple ways: as the pure surging up of the graphic event, as the expression of a magical functionality corresponding to a lived experience that is unknown to us, or as the aleatory modification of a stone landscape. It is art for us because we can see it as something other than art, because nothing allows us to know if it was painted for that reason, or if the very idea of the artist was even conceivable for the one who made it. The aesthetic affect—the affect proper to the aesthetic regime—is bound to this breaking of every direct line between cause and effect. It is tied to what we might call the impropriety of art. What touches us in contemporary art is always, as far as I am concerned, of the same order, this same straddling of several possible sensible statuses, and ultimately the straddling of the border between what is art and what is not art. And I would say that the political effect of art is tied to this indetermination as well. You see, for example, the role currently played by the blurring of the lines between documentary and fiction. A filmmaker like Pedro Costa films, in sumptuous colors, the way a group of immigrants and marginal figures (in a slum that is being destroyed on the outskirts of Lisbon) put into words what happens to them (*Vanda's Room, Colossal Youth*). Another filmmaker, Chantal Akerman, films the US-Mexico border both as a material reality and as an object of discourse (*From the Other Side*), while never representing for us either the crossing of the border or the life of immigrants in the US. The photographer Sophie Ristelhueber photographs timeless eastern landscapes in Palestine where small rockslides on the roads that seem to be accidents of nature are in fact blockades made by colonists and the Israeli army (*West Bank*). All three oppose the singular ridges of a landscape of the sensible to all the forms of banalization unleashed by the regime of information and explanation [*explication*] as well as by the regime of commiseration: they use the aesthetic affect in order to redraw, with the relations of the visible and the sayable, the frontiers of the tolerable and the intolerable as well as those of the possible and the impossible.

In the "Preface" to the *Grundrisse*, Marx states that the art of the Greeks still affects us and that it still offers us "pleasure" and remains a "norm" and a "model." What importance would you give to this remark?

JR: I don't think there is any reason to give it a great deal of importance. Marx poses the question in terms of survival: why does the old subsist in the new that wants to abolish it? Why do we still take pleasure in works left to us by a mode of production and a society that we no longer have anything to do with? He was actually more inspired when he spoke of the necessity of donning Roman clothes when making the "bourgeois" revolution. The old does not survive in the new. The new is, in fact, a repetition, a taking up again, a transformation of our relation to the old. For Racine's contemporaries, the works of the ancient tragedians were models, and the "copies" made of them were adapted to the sensibility of the century, but no one would have thought of actually staging them.

With Winckelmann and his successors, the recourse to an "authentic" Greece transformed its status, opposing a "living" Greece to the tamed Greece of the century of Louis XIV. But this living Greece is itself multiple: the Greece of democratic freedom and the Greece of Dionysian suffering. And this multiplication of significations is shadowed by a multiplication of temporalities: the art of ancient freedom is at the same time very near us and yet lost forever. Lost forever, but the very presence of these monuments of freedom in our midst promises us a future where freedom will "once again" be inscribed in the sensible tissue of existence, where art and life will be identical. It is this multiplication of antiquities that creates breaches in the distribution of forms of sensible experience. This is what allows for multiple appropriations.

When speaking of your method of analysis of the aesthetic regime, you refer to Kant, but your work is also marked by a discussion of Foucault. Roughly: an aesthetic in Kant's sense, but reworked by Foucault. What does this mean for you? To what extent can what you call a "distribution" be aligned with what Foucault calls a historical a priori? And would you agree that the difference between your project and that of Foucault is critical, insofar as you accord art the possibility of intervening on the edges of these a priori?

JR: There is no doubt that the notion of the distribution of the sensible and the classification of the regimes of identification of the arts owe a great deal to the Foucauldian notions of the episteme and the historical a priori. For me and for him, it is a matter of defining conditions of possibility for an experience either of forms of articulation between words and things or between forms of enunciation and modes of sensible presentation of the "objects" these enunciations concern. My way of thinking the historical emergence of art as a unifying category in its difference with the distribution of the arts is similar to his way of thinking the emergence of life with regard to the tableaux of natural history. My perspective is distinguished from his, however, insofar as I am more sensitive to what a regime of perception and thought allows for than to what it forbids, to what it brings together and makes circulate than to what it excludes. The fundamental intuition that sustains Foucault's conceptualization is that power classifies, orders, forbids, excludes and that, even when it authorizes, it does so in the form of a constraint (see *The History of Sexuality: The Will to Know*, where the demand for free speech is transformed into an obligation to speak imposed by power); his is an intuition of exclusion, of an inside structured by the outside, of reason constructed on the basis of the confinement of madness. This is why, for him, an episteme is a structure that invalidates certain possibilities of enunciation: a new episteme means that there are things you can no longer say, things that you can no longer think. My fundamental intuition is that of equality, that is, of the dispersion and multiplication of capacities and possibilities. A new regime of perception and thought is first of all for me a new form of inclusion, a regime of complication. One regime does not annul another: the representative logic is preserved at the heart of the aesthetic regime; it penetrates the new arts like cinema while being invalidated among older arts like painting and writing. And the ethical logic of identification between artistic performances and collective forms of life ceaselessly chips away at it and presents itself as its ultimate end: art that surpasses its particularity in order to become a common, lived world. In short, the conditions of possibility of one regime are not a priori ones that define an age. What is called artistic modernity is thinkable on the basis of new forms of visibility and intelligibility proper to the aesthetic regime. But these new forms do not themselves define any particular content: the possibility of abstract painting is inscribed in the continuous, century-long knotting of the visible and words that changed the visibility of the figurative tableau. It is the modification of the gaze cast on Rembrandt, Rubens, Titian or Chardin that created the visibility of the tableau as an abstract composition of movements and colors. Art does not intervene on the edges of historical a priori: it contributes to the interlacing of temporalities that constitutes all history. A form of the distribution of the sensible or a regime of art is never identical to this or that era.

Let's move on to the writing of history. Is it possible to write the history of a regime with respect to its conditions? What is history? Why and how does one write on or about history? Is a history of breaks, of subjectivations, of disputes [*litiges*] in your sense of the term, possible?

JR: A history is always, first of all, the putting to work of a certain regime of historicity: a specific idea about what makes history, that is, also of who makes history. The "histories" that coincide with the ethical and representative regimes are the histories of those whose actions make history and offer examples to be imitated. The model is that of Plutarch's *Parallel Lives*, which Vasari and his followers took up again in order to give painters and sculptors dignity, and to subtract them from the life without history of artisans. The aesthetic regime emerges with another notion of history: history as a form of collective life, a mode of coexistence that brings together the illustrious and the obscure, the objects of daily life and the monuments of public life. History, such as the concept was imposed at the end of the eighteenth century, is a new mode of historicity. It is the category of collective life that suppresses the difference between those who make history and those who do not. Now, it is through art and literature that this new concept of history as a collective process is imposed: it circulates among historians of art like Winckelmann, philosophers like Hegel, and novelists like Sir Walter Scott and Victor Hugo before defining a new idea of politics and landing, finally, at the feet of historians. But saying that history is a category and a horizon of collective life is also to say that it has no content of its own. History does not exist as an oriented course of development, it exists through the singular forms of historicity: the singular ways that the distributions of the visible and the sayable, the distributions of the modes of sensible experience, and the relations between life and its systems of symbolization are displaced. For me, there can only be a history of singularities. Now, a singularity is precisely a form of disappropriation, of dis-identification. This can be a certain form of subjectivation. For example, in *The Nights of Labor*, I studied the mode of subjectivation that, in the nineteenth century, constituted the core of worker emancipation: what happens there is, first and foremost, a change in perspective. Workers make themselves another body than the one that assigns them a certain place, that of production and reproduction without history. They fashion for themselves disinterested, aesthetes' gazes, they appropriate the language of poets, the modes of argumentation practiced by those who participate in public life, and so on.

A singularity can be a mutation in the gaze or look: when Hegel looks at Murillo's paintings of beggar boys in Munich, he sees in them the equals of the noble statues of Greek gods and heroes celebrated by Winckelmann. When the Goncourts describe a painting by Chardin, they transform the plates, tablecloths or fruits represented into events of pictorial matter. When Zola writes *The Ladies' Delight* or *The Belly of Paris*, he contributes to the invention of a new beauty: the beauty of shop displays. When Chaplin's contemporaries describe his art, they fix the status of the cinema as an instrument realizing an old dream or old paradox: the art of the sentient automaton.

A singularity can be a name or a concept that exceeds the object it is supposed to designate. The aesthetic regime of art is also the history of those names that "disappropriate" themselves: painting is not only an art, in the sense of a know-how that produces works called paintings, it is the idea of the power of the visible and of mutations of its relations to the order of significations. Cinema and photography are both ideas of light and of movement as generators of a new sensible environment; dance is the idea of the relation between art performance and the attitudes of the community, etc. I am currently working on a history of the aesthetic regime of art that would be just this: not a history of art or the arts, but a history of aesthetic singularities. That is, how a description of a statue or painting, the story of a play or the spectacle of a dance, the critique of a cinematographic performance define mutations in the relations between the visible and speech, narrative, drawing and gesture, the room and the stage, the place of art and its outside.

What is at stake in your work between and among the milieus of politics, philosophy and aesthetics? How can the relations between examples—let's take Blanqui and Agrippa—and theory be defined?

JR: What is primarily at stake is the contestation of the distributions that confine this or that question to politics, philosophy, sociology or aesthetics. Historical singularities are never disciplines. They are always ways of breaking the order of disciplines, the distribution of territories, the systems of authorization and interdiction weighing on objects of thought. This is how I have been able to think a singularity like worker emancipation, by refusing the immense gap that is supposed to separate philosophy from social history, and by directly confronting Plato's statements on the division of labor and the distribution of metals and souls with the worker texts that speak to us of the "same thing." Plato explains to us why the artisans should remain where they are, and not concern themselves with politics or poetry or thinking: because "work does not wait." This "obvious" empirical fact is clearly a symbolic distribution where "time" is the basis of an exclusion. The worker texts I worked on confirm this "duplicity" of time as an empirical given and as a symbolic exclusion, and they allow us to think emancipation as a rupture of this logic of time that is much more profound than the famous fable of shooting out the clocks. In order to understand what is at stake in emancipation you have to break the distribution of disciplines. This epistemological imperative is also a political one. To posit thought as something that denies the separations among philosophical argumentation, historical explanation and literary statement is to define it as a power shared by just anyone [*n'importe qui*]. Fundamentally, there are two logics: the one that divides thought into specific competences and domains for specialists, who fragment it into differences that are the small change of a principled inequality; or the logic that thinks it as an undivided power, similar in all of its exercises, shareable among anyone or whoever [*n'importe qui*]. My vision of philosophy is first of all a vision of thought as a power of declassification, of the redistribution of territorial divisions among disciplines and competences. Philosophy says that thought belongs to all. It says this, though, at the very moment that it states division and exclusion. In order to decree a correspondence between a distribution of souls and distribution of conditions, Plato must have recourse to a mode of discourse that refutes all hierarchy: he tells a story.

The pertinence of a concept is inseparable from the construction of a scene, a staging, and it is this thought that governs my use of "examples" that are, in fact, not examples. My examples stage the distribution, that is, the immanence of the division in the community that the universal of the definition declares and, inversely, the common power of language and thought in the staging of the difference of capacities. Let's take the example of the Plebeian secession to the Aventine and Menenius Agrippa's intervention as it is put to work in *Disagreement*. At the beginning, it is necessary to underline this: the Aristotelian definition of the political animal as an animal endowed with the logos is in fact the opening of a polemical space where it is a matter of knowing who really knows how to use the human logos and who is capable of discerning what he is doing. For the patricians, the plebeians do not speak because they are beings without names. Only noise comes out of their mouths. The plebeians must prove that they speak and therefore that they must be engaged with. In Titus Livius's account, Menenius Agrippa simply reminds the plebeians that they are the passive belly of the social body whose active members are the patricians. But in the version I chose, that of the French philosopher Ballanche, he uses this scene to show his colleagues that the supposedly "mute" do in fact speak. I chose his version because it is exactly contemporaneous with the French revolution of 1830 and the emergence of worker emancipation. This allows one to see how a matter of conceptual "definition" can be the staging of a distribution of the sensible whose stakes—who does or does not exercise the common power of language and thought?—are immediately implied in a political overturning and in the mutation of the perceptions of the dominated. In the same way, I proposed thinking the emergence of the aesthetic through exemplary scenes like the face-to-face with the Juno Ludovisi in Schiller, because the scene allows us to measure what is at stake in the position of the aesthetic relation as thought of thought and as thought of the community. In the narrative or theoretical construction of the scene, the distribution of the sensible is put into play by a notion, an explanation or the constitution of a territory of objects and a mode of rationality.

Another central concept in your texts is subjectivation. How is a subjectivation thinkable? Can you elaborate the relation between this concept of subjectivation as what unfolds through breaks and ruptures, and the notion of disincorporation that you also use? In what way is this notion related to sensible experience? Sticking with the question of subjectivation, we would also like to know how you distinguish between subject and subjectivation. Should subjectivation always assume a figure or can it be thought of as permanent?

JR: The notion of subjectivation refers to a set of operations, and it defines a subject only in the relation between these operations and what they produce. A political subjectivation is the constitution of a collective statement and manifestation or demonstration. It can declare itself using the name of a subject—"we, citizens," "we, workers," "we, women"—but the political subjects thus defined only exist in the relation between the pronoun and the noun, in the difference between them, and in the opposition that this difference brings out with regard to every form of identity assumed by a real group defined by a common social belonging. This is what opposes the political to what I call the police: the police is the regime of identity and the calculus of identities, the symbolic constitution of a society as a set of defined and identifiable groups. This is why a subjectivation is always a dis-identification. "We, citizens" separates itself from the collectivity of citizens defined simply by a national belonging; "we, women" separates itself from the collectivity of women defined in terms of the distribution of identities and sexual functions. A foreigner should always be able to come among "citizens," a masculine individual among "women," the son of a wealthy family among "workers." This is where the disincorporation and its sensible aspect come in. The constitution of the "we, workers," for example, meant that worker singularities separated themselves from the collective identity of those who were subjected to the existence of waged, manual labor. And this separation occurred through sensible ruptures with a certain body, the body that was adapted to this condition of dependence. In my book *The Nights of Labor*, I demonstrated these properly speaking sensible transformations of a worker body that dislodges this body from its place in the police distribution of social and functional places into a new body, now disadapted to this place. This happens, for example, through a dissociation of the hand and the gaze: in a series of texts by a carpenter, we see how he constitutes a space of freedom for the gaze at the very heart of a workspace constrained by the arms. He confirms, in other words, Kant's analytic of the beautiful: we must, in order to appreciate the form of a palace, leave aside the question of knowing how much of the people's sweat was necessary to construct the privileges of the rich. He adds, in opposition to the entire tradition of what will be called critical sociology, that it is the possibility of a "disinterested" gaze that emancipates the worker. It is the dissociation of the worker body that permits the constitution of a "voice of the workers." This voice is won through the rejection of a "worker speech" and of "popular culture." A form of subjectivation is constructed through a multiplicity of sensible micro-events that break the alignment of the sensible body to a symbolic body. From a certain body it is necessary to draw out the possibility of other bodies that are potentially there: this is the heart of the aesthetic dimension of the political and this is what has strongly tied political emancipation to experimentations with new powers of the sensible proper to the aesthetic regime of art.

It is clear that there is no permanence to the forms of subjectivation as such. This does not mean that the political would only consist in the emergence of singularities with no links among them. Forms of subjectivation produce modifications of the common tissue: forms of organization, new spaces for the demonstration of dissensus, new possibilities of enunciation; they determine new combinations of temporalities. Parties and political organizations make up part of this changing landscape but precisely only as possibilities for new forms of subjectivation in a modified common world, not as permanent subjects. What remains, but moving all the while, are spaces of possible subjectivation, where new forms of subjectivation are elaborated. This is the space of a micropolitics that neither complements nor substitutes for the politics of collectives: it is the element of their transformation.

If you say that we are always among many bodies and that for you there is no big Other, would you say that your thought is a thought of immanence? Or, to phrase the question differently, is there a Rancièrian aesthetics and in what way is it different from a Deleuzian aesthetics?

JR: You can certainly consider my thought to be a thought of immanence. To speak of the distribution of the sensible is to define a common landscape, a certain knotting of sense as sensible presentation and of sense as a mode of intelligibility. It is also to define a milieu or environment that is made up of alterations, incorporations and disincorporations, of identifications and dis-identifications, of lines of temporalities that weave together, overlap and separate. This is opposed, for me, to all the substitute transcendences that populate the field of contemporary philosophy: the impact of the event, the messianic advent, the face of the Other, the presence of specters, etc. In this sense, I perhaps feel close to Deleuze's thought, with the exception that Deleuzian immanence is itself a principle of ontological difference, a transcendence that makes you pass over to the other side, to the truth of being. I am thinking of what Deleuze calls the encounter with "Primary nature" from which one returns with "bloodshot eyes" (*Essays Critical and Clinical*[3]) or of the work of art that splits your head in order to insert a Sahara within it (*Logic of Sensation*[4]). What he calls a Sahara is properly speaking a truth regime of the sensible, a power of life that is opposed to the organic and instrumental capture of bodies. For me, there is no Sahara, no process of indifferentiation. There is no metamorphosis, there are alterations. For Deleuze, art is an ontological operator, it makes the states of the body pass over into the non-organic truth of life: in

Kafka's terms, there is actually a human organism that undergoes a metamorphosis into a cockroach. In a Hitchcock film that shows a character with his leg in a cast (*Rear Window, Vertigo*), there is truly an ontological blockage of "sensori-motor logic." *In Search of Lost Time* is the spider web of a schizophrenic torn between paranoia and erotomania. For me, the broken leg or Jimmy Stewart's vertigo do not refer to ontological conversions. They are both elements in the logic of the "sensori-motor" linkage of the narration and the discovery of its hidden secret, and a way of setting up the tension between the two logics—of linking, of rupture—that is proposed by the flow of cinematographic images. Proust's book is not a nervous system or the web of a predatory insect: it is the product of a contradictory operation, a tension between two "truths": a truth that is discovered through the elimination of errors, through the erring itinerary of a search, and a truth that imposes itself, through the impact of what is not willed.

In short, for Deleuze as for me, the "aesthetic" is the thought of art as the construction of an exceptional sensorium. But for Deleuze this sensorium is an ontological difference. For me, it is only a poetic or pragmatic difference: Proust, Hitchcock or Kafka construct in some way the ontology that sustains their artistic propositions. But this ontology is only a fiction: the punctual construction of a sensorium that presents itself as a fragment detached from a sensible world that only exists in reality in the open and inexhaustible collection of these inventions. For Deleuze, there is a veritable heterogenesis. For me, there is a singular conjunction of heterogeneous sensible regimes. The Proustian narrator lives in two heterogeneous sensible worlds: the world in which the sensible impression is the impact of the true and the world in which the sensible impression is an index in an interrogation of the trustworthiness of signs. While I describe aesthetic processes in terms of operations of joining or linking [*raccord*[5]] —between words and things, the visible and narration, determination and indetermination, art and non-art, etc.—Deleuze describes them as becomings and metamorphoses.

It seems to us that you share a great deal, above all when it comes to questions concerning the aesthetic regime, with Walter Benjamin. Benjamin, for his part, was convinced that history is a dangerous space of unfulfilled possibilities. In the fourteenth thesis on the concept of history, he calls history an "object of a construction" that can actualize the past. Fashion, Benjamin writes, "has an eye for what is up-to-date, wherever it moves in the thicket of what was." History cites the past just as fashion cites the dress of another time. How does your project relate to Benjamin's philosophy of history? Can we say that Benjamin collects the political traces lurking in sensual details?

JR: There is no doubt that I share with Benjamin a critique of the linear conception of time. This critique in his work is nourished by different sources than in mine, though: he perceives political and revolutionary action as the conflagration of several times. Benjamin interpreted in a positive manner Marx's ironic remark that the French revolutionaries undertook the bourgeois revolution in Roman clothes. I have, for my part, combated the evolutionist tradition that defines the proletarian as the worker formed by large-scale industry and given the word "proletarian" back its untimely charge: proletarian is an old Latin word that fell out of favor from antiquity on and to which modern worker combatants gave a polemical power. The proletarian, in the police order, is "someone who puts down roots," the naked living being that is excluded from the symbolic order. As a political name, the proletarian is the one who must fight in order to his affirm his place within it. Benjamin also transposes, in political terms, the duplication of times that is one of the great inventions of literature: the shock of the "now-time" within the homogenous current of history is something Benjamin took both from Proust and from the surrealist promenade that awakens the city's past—its unconscious—as a bearer of promises still awaiting their realization. "Try to solve the enigma of happiness I offer you" is what the sensation surging up from the past says to the narrator in Proust. It is this very same formula that Benjamin applies to the collective past. I only share this vision of history as the presence of several times in a single time, against the linearity of the progressive vision of history or the historians of "mentalities" that define a period of time as a homogenous totality. No future without the presence in the present of the past as suffering and as promise, borne by things, written on walls, signified by images of bodies. I cannot, in turn, support the third component of his thought of time, which reinterprets this presence of many times in one through the categories of redemption and the messianic present. There again, I oppose the work of alterations and the interweavings of temporality to the brusque appearing of the Other. To the thought of the state of exception and of the salvation that can come only from the extreme limit of despair, I oppose the power of hope and of action drawn from the perception of the absence of any historical necessity and from the recognition of the contingency of all domination and of the potentials as yet still unknown borne by the intelligence shared by all.

A question concerning one of your teachers, with whom you wrote a book and from whom you later distanced yourself, once again with a book: your critique of Althusser concerns his relation to the masses. Would you agree that this relation undergoes a change in the later Althusser, above all through his reading of Spinoza? This change can be found, perhaps, in the concept of aleatory materialism, which proposes in turn the thought of a new relation between science and ideology. A new relation that is, primarily, a relation of permanent conflict. In short, what is the importance of the Althusserian legacy for you?

JR: The Althusserian legacy can only be, for me, the legacy of classical Althusserianism: the will to refound Marxism, by simultaneously separating oneself from the economistic and evolutionist tradition of the communist parties and from the humanist and existentialist traditions that were a response to it, and by reinterpreting Marxism in light of what the structuralist thinkers made possible: new ways of thinking collective forms of life, the relations between objective necessities and singular emergences or ruptures between temporalities. In passing, I can say that the Althusserian legacy is also an invention of this concept of structuralism that brought together, in the name of a common distance from both of these traditions I cite, fairly heterogeneous theories. But this invention was produced in the name of a new form of scientism that disqualified de facto, as ideological, the political action that it itself called for insofar as it refuted the evolutionist thesis. Althusserianism, for me, is this unstable theoretico-political compromise that marked a generation in a contradictory way, by giving rise to both the thought of a radical rupture and the thought of its infinite deferral. That Althusser later evolved, that he more or less supported the Deleuzo-Marxism forged by Negri through the overlapping of an expanded Marxist concept of the development of the productive forces and Deleuzian vitalism—this is a matter of his individual intellectual history, not the historical impact and legacy of his thought.

At the end of *Disagreement*, you argue that the political has become more and more rare in the age of nihilism. How can this diagnosis be distinguished from the metapolitical statement that the political has disappeared? Is there a return to the political? In short, and to speak like Lenin, what must be done?

JR: The theme of the end of the political actually declares the end of a specific political sequence: it declares the end of the politics that gives itself the task of emancipating the oppressed. It is for this very reason, moreover, that it can declare itself in turn to be a return to the political, that is, a return to the political conceived as the business of an enlightened elite that is alone capable of perceiving problems common to all and providing their solutions. Behind these slogans that are apparently opposed but have the same content, there is a simple fact: the growing weight of a consensus. The word consensus signifies a great deal more than a "modern" form of government that gives priority to expertise, to arbitration and to the negotiation between "social partners" or different types of communities in view of avoiding conflict. Consensus signifies an accord between sense and the senses, that is, between a sensible mode of presentation and a regime of interpretation of these sensible givens. It signifies that, whatever divergence there might be among our ideas and aspirations, we perceive the same things and accord them the same signification. As a logic of government, consensus says: there are differences of interest, value and aspiration within our population. But there is an objective reality whose self-evidence imposes itself universally on all, and poses the same problems for everyone. The context of economic globalization allows for the imposition of an image of a world where the problem for each national collectivity is to adapt itself to a self-evident fact over which it has no hold, to adapt its labor market and forms of social protection to this fact. The entire combined efforts of states and international organizations today is moving in the direction of imposing this treatment of common affairs as problems that can be made entirely objective, and which require the calculations of experts. And this movement is supported by a powerful intellectual offensive that assimilates the forms of struggle against the "necessities" of the market both to defensive reactions of groups defending their archaic privileges against the necessity of progress and the extension of the power of the commodity and as inevitable consequences of democratic societies and mass individualism. Confronted with this, political action is no doubt in a difficult situation, but it is in no way changed with regard to its principle, which is precisely to declare the litigious, polemical character of all such "facts." This is indeed what happens a little bit everywhere, on the national or international level, when movements of struggle contest this or that aspect of this "global objective necessity": the liquidation of "social guarantees," the establishment of "tolerance thresholds" for immigration, wars for the geopolitical remodeling of the world, etc. It is indeed true that the convergence of these movements is for the moment difficult. The "internationalism" practiced by the powerful tends to isolate these combats, and the difficulty encountered in imagining a future free of market domination following the collapse of the soviet hopes forces these movements back onto their single, punctual objective. But this is precisely the right occasion to rethink the question "what is to be done?" in other terms: no longer "what end should we pursue?" but what capacity should be put to work? We could answer: what we can do is undertake in every circumstance the valorization of the contingency of necessity and the capacity of those deemed "incompetent." We don't know what might come of this. But we do know that it is only in this way that a future that is worth the effort can come to pass.

How would you describe the importance of Deleuze's thought for you and for your texts?

JR: My relation to Deleuze cannot be described in terms of influence. Deleuze had, in fact, no role in the constitution of my interests, my ways of feeling and my manner of problematizing objects of reflection. For a long time, I read him very little and understood absolutely nothing: understanding an author, for me, means being able to do something with what he says, to appropriate it for myself and to reinvent it. Whatever Deleuze and Foucault might say, concepts not tools. A tool is supposed to serve anybody and everybody equally, and the tools of philosophy really only serve themselves: the perfect vacuity of so many writings that "use" "tools" left by Deleuze, Foucault, Althusser or Derrida teach us this every day. Concepts are rather ways to make a relief of a particular terrain, of tracing lines between this point and that one, of drawing a territory. They materialize, then, first of all the manner of "going" to a terrain, of linking the work of words on words to the drawing of this "exterior" of this other that words themselves convoke. The way Foucault had of penetrating into the heart of a certain distribution of sensible experience by cutting through the library and the archive—which brings together the environments, noises and wounds of the social world through these yellowed papers, and allows them to be perceived as a sensible flavor and as the operative power of words that describe, classify, order—is a way of making concepts that I can use and appropriate. It corresponds to my own sensibility, to my taste for rupture, distance, my attention to the configuration of a landscape at once conceptual and lived in, the sense of what words without thickness do to things said to be concrete. To the contrary, Deleuze's way of performing a coalescence of the key words of metaphysics and the monsters that inhabit dreams and myths, this convergence that carries us off into the power of Life, describes a metaphysical imaginary within which I cannot find my place. Finally, I arrived at Deleuze's thought through the urging of others: those who, after Deleuze's death, asked non-Deleuzians and anti-Deleuzians to contribute to the evaluation of his thought. And also by students who asked me to "direct" theses on a writer they had read more of than I had. From this point on, I found myself compelled to enter into a dialogue with Deleuze's thought. I can summarize this dialogue by saying that Deleuze belongs, for me, among those philosophers who wanted to expand philosophy, to give it a constructive role with regard to what is called its objects, to introduce philosophy's outside into the very heart of philosophy. This thought is therefore a fundamental reference point for my own project, which is, to the contrary, to make philosophy take leave of itself, to introduce its procedures, propositions, arguments and descriptions in the topography of a wider territory, populated by inventions of thought, where it can encounter the words of writers and the montages of filmmakers, but also the inventions of language and thought undertaken by those who are not counted as thinkers. At the point where these two projects—whose scope is not comparable—intersect, there are certain domains and operations that are privileged: notably the operations of alteration, defiguration and indifferentiation that make up the domain of art and aesthetic experience in the aesthetic regime of art. As I said earlier, I try to describe these operations as inventions, the creation of modes of visibility, the constitution of new ways of being affected, etc., whereas Deleuze sends these operations into the realms of ethology and metaphysics. When describing the double narrative logic at work in Proust, the "thwarted fable" in Hitchcock's films or the transformations of visibility in the genre painting of the eighteenth century, I must oppose my analyses of these operations to Deleuze's becomings and metamorphoses. Deleuze is therefore for me an essential point of reference not because he provides me tools I can use, but because he allows me to understand what I do with the same "objects" that he treats, what world I construct for them: not that of the manifestation of the excessive power of life but that of the verification of the equality of intelligences.

What do you think of the divisions between science, philosophy and art as they are found in Deleuze's work? Deleuze spoke of art in terms of the production of percepts and defined the work of philosophy as the construction of concepts. Would you agree with this distinction? Or, how would you distinguish your understanding of the intersection of politics and aesthetics from that of Deleuze?

JR: What makes answering so difficult is that I do not think that Deleuze, in his mode of argumentation or writing, observes the distinctions he himself asserts. The "plateaus" that make up *A Thousand Plateaus* are aesthetic creations, composed of stagings and sensible landscapes as much as they are conceptual creations. And, correlatively, many artistic percepts that he evokes are in fact only statements: I am thinking, for example, of the insect squeaking of Gregor Samsa in *The Metamorphosis*. Kafka recounts it, Deleuze acts as if we hear it, as if everything named through the speech of a writer—these squeaks, the wall of the white whale in *Moby Dick*, or the deep voice of the heroine of *Pierre, or the Ambiguities*—were a sensible reality perceived by us. And when he analyzes films, he includes commentaries on the films in the description of the type of images to which they belong. The common nature of scientific functions, philosophical concepts and artistic percepts or affects—that is, their common character as forces taken from chaos in order to impose grids on this same chaos—tends constantly to erase their differences. This is also what characterizes his apprehension of the relation between aesthetics and politics. The "vibrations" or the "clinches" that constitute works of art are directly, for Deleuze, the manifestation of the "constantly renewed suffering of men and women, their re-created protestations, their constantly resumed struggle."[6] For him, there is no isolatable political scene, no scenes of subjectivation that can be isolated. The "people" that "is still missing" will always turn up missing. It will never be possible to draw out this people from the population of percepts and affects that define suffering, protest and struggle as a great music of collective being. Art and politics are taken together, undifferentiated, in a grand ethology: histories of tribes, riots, nomadic movements, clinches, territorializations and deterritorializations, etc. In my conception, aesthetics and politics are no doubt mixed with each other: there is an aesthetics of politics since politics concerns first of all what one sees, what one says, and what one can do about it. There is a politics of aesthetics, because aesthetics creates forms of community, ruptures in the perceptual order, overturnings of sensible hierarchies. But, precisely, the aesthetics of politics and the politics of aesthetics do not meld into a single reality: thus, the art of the aesthetic regime has its own democracy, but the latter tends to perform an equality of sensible micro-events on a scale that is not the same as the constitution of the collective subjects of politics. Between the democracy of pre-human, impersonal individuations and the great undertakings of new sensible communities, the "populations" that art brings together are always missing or in excess with relation to those that manifest themselves in political collectives. Deleuze's vibrations and clinches tend to annul this excess and this default, absorbing the political into art and art into ethology. I try, for my part, to think the tensions that ceaselessly bring them together, sometimes confusing them, and often separating them.

Translated by Jason E. Smith.

1 Jacques Rancière, *The Politics of Aesthetics: The Distribution of the Sensible,* trans. Gabriel Rockhill (London: Continuum 2004), 13.

2 [I have, for the most part, translated the *partage* of Rancière's "partage du sensible" as "distribution," in accordance with what has become a standard, if inadequate, translation. It should be kept in mind that this term suggests at once what is shared and what is divided, a taking part and a taking apart. On occasions, I translate the term differently in order to exploit this duplicity—JES.]

3 Gilles Deleuze, *Essays Critical and Clinical,* trans. Daniel W. Smith and Michael A. Greco (Minneapolis: University of Minnesota Press, 1997), 79-84; 3.

4 Gilles Deleuze, *Francis Bacon: The Logic of Sensation,* trans. Daniel W. Smith (Minneapolis: University of Minnesota Press, 2004), 71.

5 [The term *raccord* used here evokes the language of the cinema and its splicing together of shots in view of "continuity." It can however, refer to any number of operations that involve the bringing together of two or more elements—JES.]

6 Gilles Deleuze and Félix Guattari, *What is Philosophy?,* trans. Hugh Tomlinson and Graham Burchell (New York: Columbia UP, 1994), 176-77.

7 [I would like to thank Rachel Kushner for her assistance in preparing the translation of this interview. —JES]

2

THE PHILOSOPHY OF (AESTHETIC) EDUCATION

Arne De Boever

In a time of economic crisis, in which education is undergoing major transformations, the philosophy of education has once again become a priority for critical thought. Starting from the question of education in Plato's *Republic,* this article discusses Immanuel Kant and Michel Foucault's competing understandings of the Enlightenment, in order to explore the legacy of their philosophies of education in the works of contemporary thinkers Jacques Rancière and Bernard Stiegler. What might be the role of aesthetics in these philosophers' different theories of education? What might be the importance of aesthetics for the philosophy of education today?

Philosophy is Education

My title appears to connect two terms that many would probably consider to be different: "philosophy" and "education." (I am also throwing in a third term, "aesthetic," to which I will return later on.) However, the position according to which philosophy and education would be different is not one that I will take up here. I would like to suggest, on the contrary, that philosophy *is* education: that it *was* and *has always been* education, since its beginnings in Ancient Greece. Obviously, I will be talking about Western, continental philosophy here—but one might be able to say the same about philosophy, or whatever the comparable "discipline" would be called, in other parts of the world. But what type of education am I talking about when I say this? What type of philosophy?[2]

I would like to start with the suggestion that philosophy is education. One can think here of Plato, generally considered to be the "father" of continental philosophy, and of his body of work. At the risk of stating the obvious, I should probably point out that Plato wrote dialogues. Many famous Athenians are featured in his work, but the most important one is undoubtedly Plato's teacher, the anti-philosopher Socrates. "Anti-philosopher" for a number of reasons (because he never wrote anything, for example), but mainly because the gist of his philosophy was that "the only thing we know is that we don't know." No wonder, one might say, that he did not take any money for his teaching! Since Socrates never wrote anything, it is of course difficult to distinguish what in Plato's thought can be attributed to Plato, and what to Socrates—but I am not going to enter into those debates here. What interests me is that in Plato, and through the figure of Socrates, philosophy originally takes the form of teaching. *Originally*, philosophy *is* education.[3]

One can see this very clearly in the first book of one of Plato's most famous dialogues, the *Republic*. It is a dialogue about justice (*dikaiosune*). It takes place at the house of an old, wealthy man called Cephalus. When Socrates asks Cephalus "what's the greatest good you've received from being very wealthy?," Cephalus replies that "wealth can do a lot to save us from having to cheat or deceive someone against our will and from having to depart for that other place in fear because we owe sacrifice to a god or money to a person."[4] Turning to the question of justice, Socrates then asks whether "we are to say unconditionally that [justice] is speaking the truth and paying whatever debts one has incurred? Or is doing these things sometimes just, sometimes unjust?"[5] It is at this point that Socrates' maddening, philosophico-educational game begins:

> I mean this sort of thing, for example: Everyone would surely agree that if a sane man lends weapons to a friend and then asks for them back when he is out of his mind, the friend shouldn't return them, and wouldn't be acting justly if he did. Nor should anyone be willing to tell the whole truth to someone who is out of his mind.[6]

Cephalus agrees that this is true, and Socrates suggests they will have to revise their definition.[7] At this point, Cephalus' son and heir Polemarchus jumps in, thus becoming the heir not just of his father's fortune but also of the argument with Socrates.

I would now like to summarize, very quickly, some of the twists and turns of the argument that follows. Polemarchus refers to the poet Simonides, who said: "it is just to give to each what is owed to him."[8] But what about the case that Socrates just cited: is one to give back whatever a person has lent to you, even if that person is now out of their mind? Polemarchus agrees that one should not. Therefore, Simonides must have meant something different than what he actually stated. Polemarchus then corrects the initial definition: "He means that friends owe it to their friends to do good for them, never harm."[9] Socrates applies this to the case he cited: "Someone doesn't give a lender back what he's owed by giving him gold, if doing so would be harmful, and both he and the lender are friends."[10] "But what about this," he asks. "Should one also give one's enemies whatever is owed to them?"[11] Polemarchus thinks one should—except that what enemies owe to each other is something bad. This produces another adjustment to the definition of justice: it is just "to give to each what is appropriate to him."[12] But what does this mean?

At this point, Socrates establishes a connection between the question of justice and "*technè*," translated as "craft." "Which of the things that are owed or that are appropriate for someone or something to have does the craft we call medicine give, and to whom or what does it give them?" "It's clear that it gives medicines, food, and drink to bodies." Now what about justice? If justice is a craft, a *technè*, what does it give, and to whom or what does it give it? Based on the previous conclusions they reached, justice "gives benefits to friends and does harm to enemies." So "to treat friends well and enemies badly is justice?," Socrates asks. "I believe so," Polemarchus replies.[13] They agree that wars and alliances are the best context to practice this type of justice. But what about justice in a time of peace? Is justice still useful then? They agree that it is: it is useful for contracts or partnerships, specifically in partnerships involving "money matters." A person is most useful in this context when money "must be deposited for safe-keeping," namely when there is no need to use the money.[14] This leads to a very negative conclusion: "justice isn't worth much, since it is only useful for useless things."[15]

A new question is then introduced: who is the person who is best at *guarding* money? Wouldn't it be some kind of thief, someone who is best at *stealing* money as well? Isn't the best doctor the one who is most able to produce diseases unnoticed? Wouldn't that mean that justice, keeping money safe, is "some craft of stealing, one that benefits friends and harms enemies?" Polemarchus violently disagrees, and returns to his original position: "to benefit one's friends and harm one's enemies is justice."[16] Once again, Socrates objects. "Surely people often make mistakes" about who is good and useful for them—they confuse their friends with their enemies and vice versa. Polemarchus agrees. By this rationale, however, "it is just for the many, who are mistaken in their judgment, to harm their friends, who are bad, and benefit their enemies, who are good." "And so we arrive at a conclusion opposite to what Simonides meant."[17] The dialogue goes on for another twenty or so pages, and concludes with Socrates saying: "Hence the result of the discussion, as far as I'm concerned, is that I know nothing, for when I don't know what justice is, I'll hardly know whether it is a kind of virtue or not, or whether a person who has it is happy or unhappy."[18]

This is not a very satisfactory conclusion… However, the ten or so pages from which I have cited so far offer a powerful instance of Socrates' pedagogical technique, his educational strategy—of what has come to be called "the Socratic method." Through a clever game of question and answer, Socrates has his interlocutors agree to a position that is opposed to the one they started with. At the beginning of the conversation, Polemarchus states that "friends owe it to their friends to do good for them, never harm"; a few pages later, he states the exact opposite: "it is just for the many, who are mistaken in their judgment, to harm their friends, who are bad, and benefit their enemies, who are good." The question of justice thus remains unanswered, at least for now.

But the *Republic* will quickly move from the question of justice at the level of the individual to the question of justice at the level of the collective, more specifically of the city-state (*polis*). Justice at this level, Socrates and his interlocutors will conclude, is a balanced distribution of classes, "everything and everyone in their right place." Return from there to the individual: justice at the level of the individual is to have a balanced distribution of the different parts of the soul. Given all of this, *politics*—which I define here, after Jacques Rancière, as the contestation of such distributions[19]—is Plato's worst nightmare. In the third book of the *Republic*, Plato famously bans poets from his city, because they can "through clever training … become anything and imitate anything."[20] Such a capacity for becoming and imitating upsets, of course, the just distribution of classes that Plato advocates. The poet is opposed to this distribution. In this sense, the poet is a profoundly political figure, a figure that challenges the inequality that is the mark of Plato's justice.[21]

From Antiquity to the Present

I would now like to make a few quick points on the basis of the reading of Plato that I developed above.

First of all, it is worth noting that the *Republic*'s conclusion, namely that justice is "everything and everyone in its right place" is profoundly un-Socratic, given that Socrates is precisely the one to question what is presumed to be the "right place" of everything and everyone.

Secondly, and going back to the intimate connection between philosophy and education with which I began, it should be noted that the *Republic*'s conclusion thus appears to go against philosophy's original, educational project, which is characterized by a perpetual questioning and a potential lack of final solutions. Although the book contains a justly famous allegory of education—the so-called allegory of the cave[22]—this allegory is counter-balanced by Plato's plea for ideologies such as the "myth of the metals,"which is designed to keep everything and everyone in its right place.[23] In Plato's allegory of education, it is presumably only the philosophers who see the light. Their task is to then return into the cave and educate those who are stuck in the shadow-world, but if one situates the allegory in context it is doubtful that this education would apply to everyone. *Not everyone should know* that the "myth of the metals" is actually a myth. Philosophers are allowed to know because they are like doctors: they can use ideological poison, "useful falsehoods"in the service of the greater good.[24]

This means, thirdly, that there are actually two competing visions or philosophies of education that clash in Plato's text. One is associated with Socrates, the anti-philosopher, who questions everything and everyone and does not reach a final solution other than the fact that "the only thing we know is that we don't know." The other is associated with the *Republic*—with Plato, if you want. It leads to the conclusion—heavily criticized by Jacques Rancière —that justice is "everything and everyone in its right place."

Considering these two positions from our twenty-first century perspective, and through the lens of twentieth-century philosophy, one could characterize this second position with reference to Louis Althusser's famous thesis about the school as an "ideological state apparatus."[25] It draws out the dark underside of the Enlightenment project, the second motto of the Enlightenment on which Michel Foucault, in his work, insists: not simply Immanuel Kant's motto "Dare to know!" but also his emphasis on obedience. The Socratic position would then be closer to Kant's: "Dare to know!": dare to confront even the abyss of the impossible conclusion that "the only thing we know is that we don't know."[26] The Delphic motto "Know yourself" should, as Foucault in his lectures on *The Hermeneutics of the Subject* recalls, be understood in this light: it is not about a positive knowledge of the self, but about an awareness of the self's limitations—it is about a critique of the self.[27] For Foucault, the task is of course to transform such a critique into a practice of transgression. That is where his late work on aesthetico-ethical practices of the self—the so-called *souci de soi* or "care of the self"—comes in.[28]

The "heroes" of such a reading of the *Republic* would be Socrates, the Kant of "Dare to know!," and perhaps also Foucault, or at least the Foucault who worked on the "care of the self." The hero of such a reading would be the Socratic method. Philosophy is education because of the Socratic method. That is where its politics also lie. *But this can only be a provisional conclusion.*

The positions that I have discussed so far return in the work of two contemporary French philosophers: Bernard Stiegler and Jacques Rancière. Stiegler's entire project can be situated along the Socrates-Kant-Foucault axis, as he himself reveals in one of his recent works, *Taking Care of Youth and the Generations.* It is particularly interesting in this context that Stiegler is currently starting a school in France that is inspired by the Socratic method. I want to argue, however, that although Stiegler's project is of course very admirable, Rancière discovers through (or perhaps better: beyond) Socrates a more radical model of education—and thus a third vision or philosophy of education—that challenges not just what Rancière calls "the distribution of the sensible"[29] in Plato's *Republic,* but also the notion of the Socratic method itself. This is most clear in his work *The Ignorant Schoolmaster.*

It is at this point that I want to bring in the third term in my title: "aesthetic." Rancière's understanding of education has in recent years developed into a political theory of aesthetics, into a theory of the politics of aesthetics as what challenges any distribution of the sensible on the basis of a radical assumption of equality. Such a challenge is already contained, although it is not yet theorized in this specific way, in Rancière's *The Ignorant Schoolmaster.* Stiegler, for his part, is currently embarking on an investigation of aesthetics. One could argue that so far, aesthetics has been limited in his work to technology; up until this point, "art" has thus equaled "*technè*" for Stiegler. It is perhaps for this reason that his view on education, his philosophy of education, also risks to remain stuck in the so-called Socratic method. Rancière opens one's eyes to another philosophy of education: one that would challenge the Socratic method itself in the name of a more democratic emancipation.

In *Taking Care of Youth and the Generations*, Stiegler explicitly raises the question "What is philosophy?"[30] His answer is that philosophy is teaching. He theorizes philosophy as teaching, specifically as teaching "understanding" (it is not about transmitting *knowledge* but about *understanding*[31]). Understanding, for Stiegler, is a practice of care-taking: of taking care of oneself and of others. Thus, philosophy is teaching is understanding is care-taking. That is the chain of identifications that Stiegler sets up. Acknowledging Foucault's critique of disciplinary power, he insists that one recalls Kant's "Dare to know!" to explore what this imperative might still mean today, in the age of technological revolution.

The polemic that Stiegler engages in involves the "mind." His book *Taking Care* and his work in general challenge the ways in which the mind has become increasingly saturated by technological developments, to the extent that the technological apparatus is in the process of destroying the mind. Humanity has not yet developed an "ecology" of apparatuses or, to come to the problem from the other side of the relation, an ecology of the mind, a "mental ecology" (to recall the notion that Félix Guattari uses in *The Three Ecologies*) that can balance these technological developments and the classical techniques of taking-care of the self.[32] Such ecologies, such practices of care-taking, can be developed, unsurprisingly given the chain of identifications that the book sets up, through understanding, which is teaching, which is philosophy. Stiegler thus turns to philosophy to confront the mind's saturation and potential destruction by technology today.

Although there is definitely (and perhaps surprisingly so for readers of Stiegler's early work on *Technics and Time*) some anxiety about technology here, Stiegler's argument is *not* an argument *against* technology. It focuses, rather, on the mind's relation to technology and the ways in which this relation can be a relation of care (as every relation, this one goes both ways: care of technology towards the mind, and of the mind towards technology). This is what it would mean to develop a *philosophy* of technology, a "technical thought" or "mentality" (as one of Stiegler's main influences, the French philosopher of technology Gilbert Simondon, has put it).[33] This position is clearly expressed in many of Stiegler's works, but perhaps most succinctly in the manifesto of an organization called *Ars Industrialis* that Stiegler started with a number of other contemporary French thinkers.[34]

Ars Industrialis is interested in what they call "technologies of the spirit"[35]—a clear reference to Foucault's technologies of the body. They are interested not so much in disciplinary power and bio-politics, but in psycho-politics. As Foucault showed, the age of technological revolutions has "brutally intensified the possibilities for the control of mind and spirit."[36] In the face of this, *Ars Industrialis* affirms "that the technologies of the spirit can and must become a new age of the spirit, that they can spark a renewal of the spirit and issue in a new 'life of the mind'."[37] So it is entirely a question of putting these technologies to a different use, of coming up with "new and original social practices that these technologies do not encourage but call for as an essential requirement"[38]: "these technologies should become the basis of a new epoch of civilization and could conduct the neutralization of the imminent threat of chaos everyone senses."[39] The age of technological revolutions has destroyed people's libido; in the new age of the spirit, the libido must be boosted. Desire must be boosted, the manifesto states, and not simply to boost consumption.

It is a powerful argument that, in books such as *Taking Care of Youth and the Generations,* is couched in a discussion of, for example, the question of "attention" in contemporary France—the way in which attention deficit disorder is characteristic of French (and not just French) children today. Stiegler links this directly to the era of technological revolutions and the destruction of the mind that it has brought. One initiative that is featured on the *Ars Industrialis* website is "Dix Jours sans Écrans," "Ten Days without Screens," as a means to reclaim the mind from these developments and open it up onto new presents and futures. This is part of a process of re-creating desire, of re-enchanting the world: the mind needs to be liberated from the tangles of technology, capitalism, consumption, and the like. A mental ecology needs to confront the potentially destructive results of these developments.

In *Taking Care,* Stiegler aligns himself in this endeavor with the Kant from "Dare to know!" The affirmative part of the book begins with a reflection on Plato and philosophy as education. It is a powerful philosophical self-situating, because it inscribes the project of *Ars Industrialis* into the inheritance of the Enlightenment within which we are still living.

Michael Hardt and Antonio Negri do the same in the opening chapters of the third installment of their trilogy *Empire-Multitude-Commonwealth.* They devote an entire section of the book to Kant's "Dare to Know!" In these pages, they distinguish between what they call—somewhat confusingly, given that Kant appears to use these same terms in a different way—the "major" Kant of "Obey!" and the "minor" Kant who "blasts apart [the republic's] foundations, opening the way for mutation and free creation on the biopolitical plane of immanence."[40] If Kant's desire to "become major" involves "obedience," they prefer the "minor" Kant, the one who challenges that obedience in the same text that he insists on it. When Hardt and Negri discuss a number of political thinkers today, including Bernard Stiegler, they situate Stiegler (without giving him any airtime) in a "third stream of interpretations of biopolitics" which in their view "lacks a dynamic character because it is closed within its invariable, naturalistic framework."[41] Stiegler, like Simondon and Sloterdijk (the two other thinkers they mention here), is too naturalistic and invariable in his politico-philosophical analysis. For this reason, "the biopolitical resistance of these invariables can never create alternative forms of life."[42] Although Hardt and Negri may be putting it a little too strongly here, there is something to their critique of Stiegler. Rather than focusing on their reproach of naturalism, I want to focus on the tension they observe between the "major" and the "minor" Kant to develop this. Stiegler clearly wants to be with what Hardt and Negri call the "minor" Kant, the one of "Dare to know!" in its most radical interpretation. But how does he interpret this "Dare to know!"? Most importantly, what does it look like in practice?

From a recent proposal for a school of philosophy that I received from Stiegler in personal correspondence—the school has in the meantime been launched, it is called the "Ecole de Philosophie d'Epineuil-le-Fleuriel"[43]—it appears that Kant's "Dare to know!" is aligned for Stiegler with the figure of Socrates and specifically with the Socratic method. Much of what is said in the proposal revolves around what Stiegler considers to be the essential philosophical question, "what is…?" (*ti esti*, in Ancient Greek). That is the question that kick-starts all Platonic dialogues: what is justice, love, politics, and so on. That is also the question that is raised in chapter seven of *Taking Care*: "What is philosophy?" It is the *ti esti* that will shape the educational project of Stiegler's proposed school of philosophy. Education and philosophy coincide in the Socratic question of the "what is…?"

All of the themes of *Ars Industrialis'* manifesto are brought together around this question. The whole project of the school will, at least in the first year of its existence, revolve around it, and around the question of the libido or the desire that it boosts—around the economy, politics, and so on to which it may lead. It appears to me that one should draw into question this centrality of the Socratic method to the project of the school, because *a simple turning to the Socratic method might actually not solve that much*. The issue will be, rather, whether the force of Socrates' questioning will be maintained, or whether it will be allowed to dissipate into the ideological structure of Plato's *Republic*.

In the split between Kant and Foucault, Stiegler has decided to go with Kant, and there is much virtue in taking up that position today. But such a jump does not necessarily achieve anything. The two competing visions of philosophy and education—"Dare to know!" and "Obey!"—ultimately risk ending up as the same, given that Socrates ultimately gives way to the "everything in its right place" motto of the *Republic*. How to stick with Socrates, with the radical mode of philosophy and education that his figure represents? How to go beyond him even, to question Socrates himself? Of this, Rancière's work on education provides an example.

Socrates versus The Ignorant Schoolmaster

I always try to think in terms of horizontal distributions, combinations between systems of possibilities, not in terms of surface and substratum. Where one searches for the hidden beneath the apparent, a position of mastery is established. I have tried to conceive of a topography that does not presuppose this position of mastery.[44]

In his book on education titled *The Ignorant Schoolmaster*, Jacques Rancière develops a powerful critique of the Socratic method. Here is how Rancière characterizes the Socratic method:

Through his interrogations, Socrates leads Meno's slave to recognize the mathematic truths that lie within himself. This may be the path to learning, but it is in no way a path to emancipation. On the contrary, Socrates must take the slave by his hand so that the latter can find what is inside himself. The demonstration of his knowledge is just as much the demonstration of his powerlessness: he will never walk by himself, unless it is to illustrate the master's lesson. In this case, Socrates interrogates a slave who is destined to remain one.[45]

Stiegler to an extent incorporates this critique when he distinguishes, in *Taking Care*, between teaching as "passing on knowledge" and "passing on understanding" (Rancière also clearly criticizes an understanding of teaching as "passing on knowledge" in this passage). But the one who is silently addressed in this passage, is Kant: the Kant of "Dare to know!" who insists on becoming major and learning to walk by yourself, without the help of the technical object of the cart, and without the help of others. You do not need a pastor, a doctor, a book to take care of you for you, Kant writes; you should learn to grab hold of your own life, to become the subject of your own life rather than to be subjected to others.

There is one problem with Kant's text, however, which is the fact that it is still telling us so. In the end, the reader is turning to Kant, the master, to tell her or him what enlightenment is, and basically what Kant replies to the reader is that he or she should not let anyone tell them; instead, they should become the subjects of their own enlightenment. That is enlightenment. But the point is self-defeating, because Kant has just told us so. The only way out of this is to apply Kant's critique to Kant himself, and thus to become the subject of Kant's text, rather than to be passively subjected to it. This might actually be the revolutionary core of Kant's text, given that he appears to invite one to undermine the obedience-clause that it includes. It is thus Kant's own text that needs to become enlightened, that needs to turn from a minor into a major text. This may be why Foucault refers to it at the beginning of his discussion of this text as a "minor text."[46]

Rancière's point against the Socratic method is similar: he argues that the Socratic method leaves power-structures intact, that it does not change anything about the master/slave relation. Socrates is the master, the one whom he interrogates is the slave. And at the end of the conversation, nothing about that distribution of the sensible has been changed. In response to this, Rancière asks his readers to imagine another Socrates, a more radical version of Socrates that would challenge this distribution—a political Socrates, so to speak, a political philosopher whose education would break with these hierarchical structures.

That other Socrates is Joseph Jacotot, the subject of Rancière's book and the "ignorant schoolmaster" that is referred to in his title. Jacotot was a French schoolteacher who, when he was driven into exile, ended up at a Flemish university, needing to teach students who did not know the language that he speaks. Rather than abandon the project, Jacotot took recourse to something that he and the students had in common. He gave them a bilingual version of Fénélon's *Télémaque*, which had the French original printed next to the Flemish translation, and without a word of explanation asked them to study both the Flemish and the French. When the students returned to him at the end of the semester to take the written exam in French, it turned out they had taught themselves French by way of their knowledge of Flemish. They could write French perfectly well.

The conclusion that Jacotot draws from this, and this is what appeals to Rancière, is that intelligence is equality—that everyone is equally intelligent. By this, Rancière does not mean that everyone is equally smart, only that everyone has an equal capacity to learn, if only they dedicate themselves to it. Most importantly, they do not need the figure of a master to "explain" things to them, to "pass on" or "transmit" knowledge to them; rather they can learn without the interference of such a figure. Think of how children teach themselves language. It is this auto-didacticism that Rancière is interested in. Of course, one can challenge Rancière's position. Jacotot still needed to give the students the text in order for them to learn. The text itself still needed to be written in order for the students to learn. There is always a dependence on a "*heteros*" within this project of "auto-didacticism." But the point is clear: what is done away with in Rancière's discussion is the master position of the Socratic method; everyone becomes the subject of her or his own education, philosophy, emancipation, rather than being passively subjected to education, philosophy, emancipation. Only such a subjectivization can constitute a true emancipation.

Already in this early work, Rancière suggests that to undertake such a process means to undertake the process of becoming an artist. If Plato bans poets from his ideal Republic, Rancière brings them back in as figures of radical emancipation:

> Each one of us is an artist to the extent that he carries
> out this double process; he is not content to be a mere
> journeyman but wants to make all work a means of
> expression, and he is not content to feel something but
> tries to impart it to others. The artist needs equality as
> the explicator needs inequality.[47]

The connection between the artist and emancipation that is glimpsed in this passage will become central to Rancière's later work, which is devoted entirely to an exploration of the politics of aesthetics. There, Rancière theorizes the aesthetic as a regime that challenges existing distributions of the sensible through the distributions of the sensible that it opposes to it. In several of his texts (in "The Politics of Literature," for example, but also elsewhere[48]) Rancière presents such a politics explicitly as a critique of the distribution of the sensible in Plato's *Republic*. He challenges the resolution to Socrates' questioning that is presented there; moreover, he questions the Socratic method, its power dynamics, and theorizes a more radical Socrates, a more democratic philosophy of education. It appears to me that this insight will be a very important one for Stiegler and *Ars Industrialis* to keep in mind, given that they are starting their school on the basis of Socratic principles.

An Unfinished Project

In short, Rancière offers us a philosophy of aesthetic education: a politics of aesthetics that is also a politics of philosophy and of education. To complete the analysis that I have begun, one would need Stiegler's theory of aesthetics, which has not been published yet. I would argue that so far, Stiegler's work on aesthetics has remained limited to a work on technology, which is certainly part of the field of aesthetics. However, to focus on technology and technics means to a certain extent to stay stuck in the very thing that one is fighting, namely the technique of Socrates' teaching, which Rancière exposes to be a technique of mastery. There is a masterful strategy at work there, a masterful technology that is being played out. Education thus remains a *technè*, a craft understood in the way that Socrates talks about it in the first book of the *Republic*.

It appears that Rancière, in his theory of education, is moving away from this, and from the master/slave position that it might imply. Stiegler, however, has—in the wake of Gilbert Simondon and other figures such as André Leroi-Gourhan—tried to do precisely this in this theory of technology. He has written about how human beings did not shape technology but how technology shaped them, how the tool is not the slave of the human being or vice versa but how both are part of a shared process of becoming—hence his insistence on intervening in this becoming, of "managing" this becoming towards a new politics of the mind. It is to be expected that these positions will shape Stiegler's theory of aesthetics as well, and one can only look forward, into the future, in order to see how this theory may influence his views on philosophy and education.

In April 2011, after I had already finished this article, Bernard Stiegler presented his theory of aesthetics in a series of three lectures given at the California Institute of the Arts, UC Irvine, and UCLA. The lectures clarified a number of the issues that I have addressed, and made it necessary for me to add this postscript. In his lectures, Stiegler clarified that the issue of aesthetics—of sensibility—is a technical issue, in the sense that it is an issue related to what Michel Foucault calls techniques of the self. To speak about sensibility today is to speak about techniques of living.

In response to a question I asked about aesthetic education, Stiegler also clarified his investment in the Platonic, or Socratic, question of the *ti esti*, the "what is." By returning to the *ti esti*, he is precisely trying to think "another Socrates" along the lines that I have tried to do here following Jacques Rancière's critique of the Socratic method. How is one to translate Socrates' *ti esti*, Stiegler asked? Can these words simply be translated by the French "qu'est-ce que" or the English "what is"? Referring to Roland Barthes' essay on Raymond Queneau's *Zazie dans le métro*, "Zazie and Literature," Stiegler proposes we translate *ti esti* using what Barthes calls Zazie's "clausule,"[49] her formula: "my ass" (*"mon cul"*). Whenever Socrates asks for example "what is justice?," he is really saying "justice my ass." The question of the *ti esti* is in other words not an ontological question about the essence of justice, but a question that keeps the question of justice forever open. In this sense, it is a question is about one's belief in justice—about one's attachment to justice, in its universality, without being able to prove this universality. To determine justice is impossible; yet justice is nevertheless constitutive of who we are, how we live, and how we live together.

Aesthetic education, as Stiegler understands it, should take care of such belief. Whatever is in question in education—justice, love, virtue, politics—therefore ultimately remains of the order of the "justice my ass." Its ass-hole is never properly filled. This is why, for Stiegler, the question of education is inextricably linked to the question of desire.

---

1 I first presented the thoughts that are gathered here as a public lecture in Anne Marie Oliver's "Art and Politics" seminar at the Pacific Northwest College of Art (PNCA) in Portland, Oregon. The text of that lecture has been revised for this publication. I am grateful to Anne Marie and to her students for their questions and comments.

2 One track that I will not pursue here is the relation of my title to Friedrich Schiller's *On the Aesthetic Education of Man*. For a recent text that addresses this particular history of aesthetic education, see Cathy Caruth, "Interview with Gayatri Chakravorty Spivak: Aesthetic Education and Globalization," *PMLA*

125:4 (2010), 1020-1025.

3 Indeed, I never fail to be impressed by the fact Socrates was Plato's teacher, who in turn taught Aristotle, who in turn taught Alexander the Great. Philosophy, education, and politics are intricately connected here.

4 Plato, *Republic*, trans. G.M.A. Grube (Indianapolis/ Cambridge: Hackett, 1992), 5.

5 Ibid., 5-6.

6 Ibid., 6.

7 Could it be that Socrates' question inspired the final scene of Nicholas Ray's *Rebel Without A Cause* (Warner Bros. Pictures 1955)? In Plato's *Republic*, Socrates and his interlocutor conclude that one should not give back a weapon to a person who has gone mad. In *Rebel Without A Cause*, Jim Stark follows this advice, but only halfway: he secretly removes the bullets from a gun before returning it to Plato, his friend who has gone mad. This has catastrophic consequences: Plato shot by the police waiting for him outside of Griffith Observatory, where this scene takes place.

8 Plato, *Republic*, 6.

9 Ibid.

10 Ibid.

11 Ibid.

12 Ibid., 7.

13 Ibid.

14 Ibid., 8.

15 Ibid., 9.

16 Ibid.

17 Ibid., 10.

18 Ibid., 31.

19 See all of Rancière's recent work on aesthetics and politics, but also his earlier *Disagreement: Philosophy and Politics*, trans. Julie Rose (Minneapolis: University of Minnesota Press, 1999).

20 Plato, *Republic*, 74.

21 Rancière has criticized Plato on this count throughout his work.

22 See Plato, *Republic*, 186-212.

23 "'All of you in the city are brothers,' we'll say to them in telling our story, 'but the god who made you mixed some gold into those who are adequately equipped to rule, because they are the most valuable. He put silver in those who are auxiliaries and iron and bronze in the farmers and other craftsmen. For the most part you will produce children like yourselves, but, because you are all related, a silver child will occasionally be born from a golden parent, and vice versa, and all the others from each other. So the first and most important command from the god to the rulers is that there is nothing that they must guard better or watch more carefully than the mixture of metals in the souls of the next generation. If an offspring of theirs should be found to have a mixture of iron or bronze, they must not pity him in any way, but give him the rank appropriate to his nature and drive him out to join the craftsmen and the farmers. But if an offspring of these people is found to have a mixture of gold or silver, they will honor him and take him up to join the guardians or the auxiliaries, for there is an oracle which says that the city will be ruined if it ever has an iron or a bronze guardian.'" (Ibid., 91-92.)

24 Ibid., 58, 91.

25 See Louis Althusser "Ideology and Ideological State Apparatus (Notes Toward an Investigation)," in *Lenin and Philosophy and Other Essays*, trans. Ben Brewster (New York/London: Monthly Review Press, 1991).

26 For a book that brings together both Kant and Foucault's essays, see Michel Foucault, *The Politics of Truth*, ed. Sylvère Lotringer (Los Angeles: Semiotext(e), 2007).

27 See Michel Foucault, *The Hermeneutics of the Subject: Lectures at the Collège de France 1981-1982*, ed. Frédéric Gros, trans. Graham Burchell (New York: Picador, 2005).

28 See Michel Foucault, *The Care of the Self: The History of Sexuality, Volume 3*, trans. Robert Hurley (New York: Vintage, 1988).

29 See, for example, Jacques Rancière, *The Politics of Aesthetics*, trans. Gabriel Rockhill (New York/ London: Continuum, 2004).

30 Bernard Stiegler, *Taking Care of Youth and the Generations*, trans. Stephen Barker (Stanford: Stanford UP, 2010), 107.

31 Ibid., 108.

32 Guattari, Félix. *The Three Ecologies*, trans. Ian Pindar and Paul Sutton (New York/London: Continuum, 2008).

33 See Gilbert Simondon, "Technical Mentality," trans. Arne De Boever, *Parrhesia* 7, 17-27.

34 The manifestoes of the organization are available in both French and in an English translation on the *Ars Industrialis* website: http://arsindustrialis.org/.

35 George Collins and Marc Crépon, Bernard Stiegler, Caroline Stiegler. "Manifesto." *Ars Industrialis* (13 November 2010), 1. http://arsindustrialis.org/node/1472

36 Ibid.

37 Ibid.

38 Ibid.; translation modified.

39 Ibid.; translation modified.

40 Michael Hardt and Antonio Negri, *Commonwealth* (Cambridge, MA: Harvard UP, 2010), 17.

41 Ibid., 58.

42 Ibid.

43 See *École de Philosophie d'Épineuil-le-Fleuriel*. 13 November 2010. http://www.pharmakon.fr/pharmakon/accueil.html.

44 Jacques Rancière, *The Politics of Aesthetics*, trans. Gabriel Rockhill (New York/ London: Continuum, 2009), 47.

45 Jacques Rancière, *The Ignorant Schoolmaster: Five Lessons in Intellectual Emancipation*, trans. Kristin Ross (Stanford: Stanford UP, 1991), 29.

46 Michel Foucault, "What is Enlightenment?," in *The Politics of Truth*, ed. Sylvère Lotringer (Los Angeles: Semiotext[e], 2007), 97.

47 Rancière, *The Ignorant Schoolmaster*, 70-71.

48 See Jacques Rancière, "The Politics of Literature," in Rancière, *Dissensus: On Politics and Aesthetics* (New York/ London: Continuum, 2010), 152-168.

49 Roland Barthes, *Critical Essays*, trans. Richard Howard (Evanston: Northwestern UP, 1972), 120.

3

THE PURLOINED PHILOSOPHER

Peter Friedl

I'd like to make a brief remark before beginning: I'm not going to go into any great detail about Jacques Rancière and will also quote as little as possible from his writings. His ideas on the "politics of aesthetics," "politics of art," diverse "regimes of art," etc., are popular enough and the English edition of *The Distribution of the Sensible* has a relevant glossary in the appendix, which even includes "equality" as "the only universal axiom of politics."[1] I'm also no longer interested in curating or commenting on myself. Instead, I will take the liberty of making a few incidental remarks and gather together fragments of a broken historical narrative.

The fact that philosophers say something intelligent when they speak about art and artists is not very surprising, at least not as surprising as the alternative. After all, a philosopher's job is to think, and he or she is paid to do so by state and private institutions. Ever since the middle classes began trying to silver-plate their fears of their own disappearance and the illiterate mob's invasion of the new void at the center of culture with, among other ways, excessive academic credentials (key terms: Master of or Ph.D. of Arts), one naturally becomes accustomed to the fact that silence is not necessarily golden. The rules of academic capitalism are acquired quickly.

But how does art deal with philosophers? From time to time it resorts to its own means and strategies, with varied success. Simply recall *The Nose of Lyotard* or *Baudrichard's Ecstasy* from the 1980s. The latter was the funny work with a gilded urinal on an ironing board and endlessly circulating water from a bucket with FIRE written on it—Hans Haacke's commentary on the Baudrillard fashion rampant at the time.

In November 1996, Jean Baudrillard performed at Whiskey Pete's Casino with the Chance Band, a group put together by Educational Complex specialist Mike Kelley. The casino is on Indian land on the California/Nevada Stateline. The hotel has 777 rooms and the bar has decent specials. Approaching Las Vegas from the southwest, it is the first casino that you pass or get stuck at, and

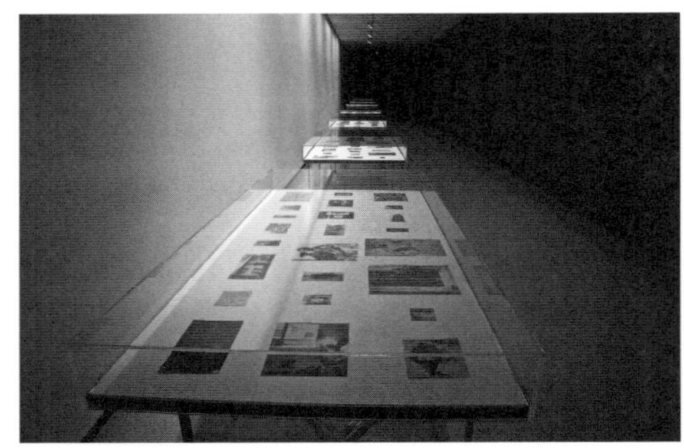

I
Peter Friedl, *Theory of Justice*, 1992–2010. Newspaper clippings and display cases. Courtesy the artist and Museo Nacional Centro de Arte Reina Sofia, Madrid. Installation view: Sala Rekalde, Bilbao. (Photo: Begoña Zubero)

II
Raphael, *The School of Athens*, 1510–11. Stanza della Segnatura, Vatican Palace, Rome.

III
Jeff Wall, *Dead Troops Talk (A Vision After an Ambush of a Red Army Patrol, near Moqor, Afghanistan, Winter 1986)*, 1991–92. Transparency in lightbox, 249 x 437 cm. Courtesy of the artist.

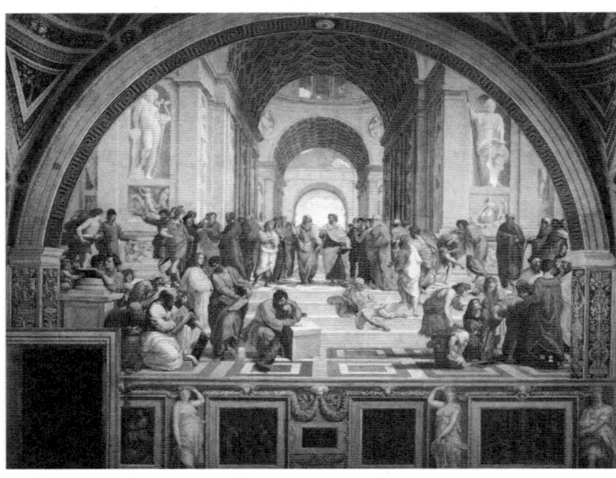

II

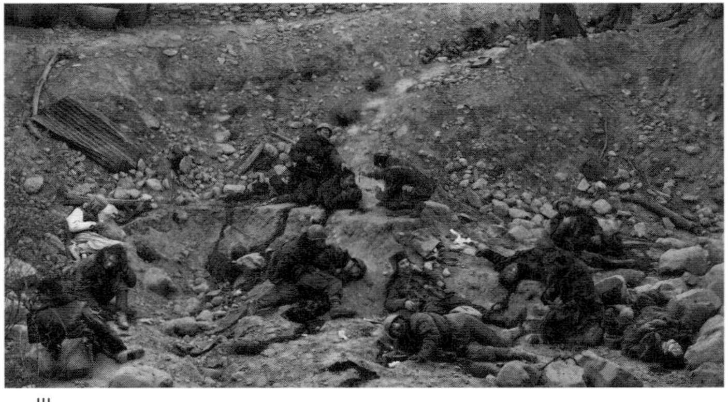

III

when leaving, it is the last. With regard to the "aesthetic educa-tion" theme, if I remember correctly, it was also in the mid-1990s that the Master of Fine Arts programs began taking off in southern California. *The Los Angeles Times* published a front-page photo of the philosopher in a gold lamé jacket. The album produced from the event in the simulated western desert is entitled *Suicide Moi.*

A philosopher also appears in *Film Socialisme* (2010), Jean-Luc Godard's latest anti-copyright-film. This time on a cruise ship (the Costa Serena) somewhere in the Mediterranean. Alain Badiou plays mainly Alain Badiou here. Godard said: "I wanted to quote Husserl's text on geometry, and I wanted someone to elaborate something of his own from that. And he was interested."[2] And why does he speak in front of an empty room?

> Because his conference didn't interest the cruise ship pas-
> sengers. We made the announcement that there would
> be a conference on Husserl and nobody came. When we
> put Badiou in this empty room, he really liked it. He said:
> "Finally, I can talk in front of no one."[3]

Probably the director himself wasn't even there. When they filmed the scene where the philosopher sits at a table with a Russian spy, at first he thought that, logically, she too, was a real spy. But she was a real actress. No doubt, Badiou cut a much better figure here than, for example, on BBC-HARDtalk on March 24, 2009, on the occasion of the international financial crisis, the coming communism, and his recently published book about Sarkozy, "the rat man."

Finally, we know that a young Giorgio Agamben—roughly one year before he completed his law studies with a thesis on Simone Weil—had a short, silent appearance as the Apostle Philip in Pasolini's *The Gospel According to St. Matthew* (1964). Not a bad internship. The seminar with Heidegger in France and his first book *The Man Without Content* came later.[4] Contemporary art does not really appear in the little book, but it is about self-nullifying, about the open wound between the artwork and aesthetic perception.

Looking for a model of artistic appropriation, exploitation, and commentary on the world of philosophers, we easily come ashore with Raphael's fresco *The School of Athens* (1510–11) in the Vatican's Stanza della Segnatura. In this *causarum cognitio* ("Knowledge of Causes"), the immortal Plato, *Timaios* in hand, has the facial features of Leonardo da Vinci, as we know them from what has been handed down. He and his no less famous student Aristotle, (with *Nicomachean Ethics* in hand) are the main protagonists in this visualization of the seven liberal arts. While Aristotle has just come to a stop, Plato is poised to complete a step, which will temporarily give him a slight lead. The brooding Heraclitus under the sign of Saturn is probably Michelangelo, and the Renaissance architect Bramante embodies Euclid (or Archimedes; there's no agreement among the painting's interpreters). The young Raphael has also not forgotten to depict himself, in the role of Apelles, ancient Greece's most famous painter (from whom not a single work has been preserved), and incidentally, close to an Iranian philosopher, the imagined-in Zoroaster.

In spite of androgyny abounding, it is purely a man's world. Even the figure that actually has to represent neo-Platonic philosopher Hypatia from Alexandria who was murdered by a Christian mob, is often interpreted as being the portrait of Francesco Maria della Rovere, the Duke of Urbino. *The School of Athens* is a rather complex narrative picture paraphrasing the basic theme of the "important conversation." Jeff Wall, who for his part with *Dead Troops Talk (A Vision After an Ambush of a Red Army Patrol, near Moqor, Afghanistan, Winter 1986)* staged a conversation of the dead or undead, once said of Raphael's fresco that its beholders must have enjoyed seeing a staged gathering of known knowledge and recognized standpoints.[5]

To put it briefly: I have no idea what should now happen with Jacques Rancière. Jacques-Louis David's *The Death of Socrates* (1787) with Roman scenography—quoting Plato's gesture of the "Theory of Forms" from Raphael's philosophical fresco—is already consumed by the mythology of the French Revolution. A long time ago we also once had the iconography of the beggar philosopher: around 1640, Velázquez painted two full-figure portraits of Aesop and Menippus. The two were freed slaves who became philosophers. Little is known about their lives. According to a dubious story handed down by Diogenes Laertius (biographer of the Greek philosophers), Menippus, usually categorized within the school of Cynics, is meant to have been a Phoenician slave who made a fortune by begging or money lending. Manet, in his three philosopher paintings created between 1864 and 1869, took up the motif and painting style of Velázquez, whom he greatly admired. His rag-picker in front of the masterly vague, indifferent background corresponds with the figure heroicized by Baudelaire, the *chiffonier* who like the poet of modern life wanders the city streets at night to the government's great disapproval.

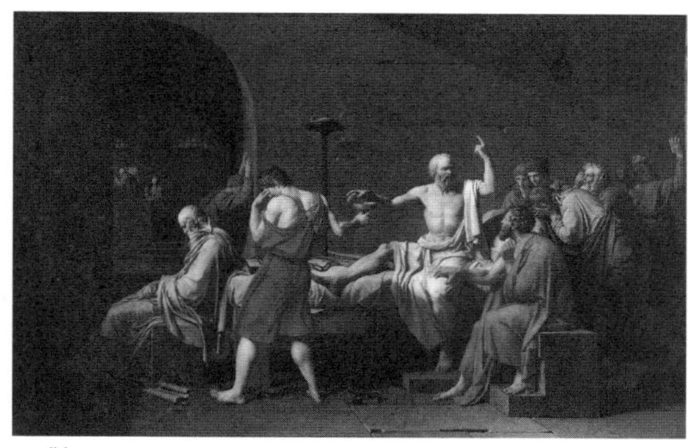

IV

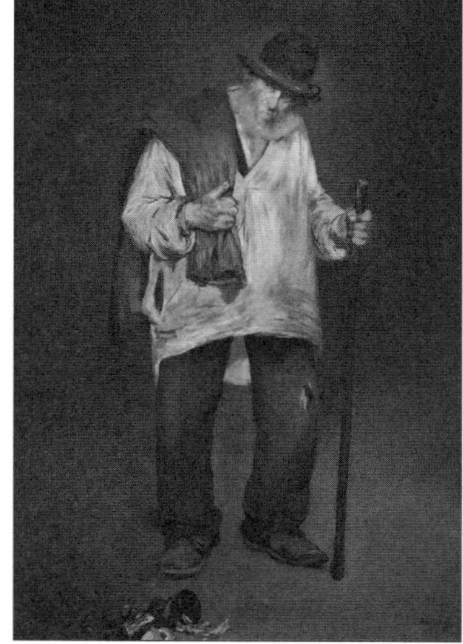

V

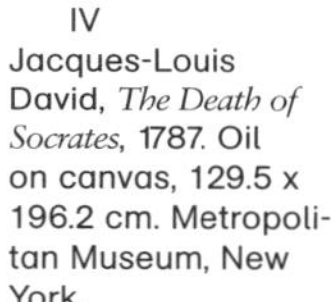

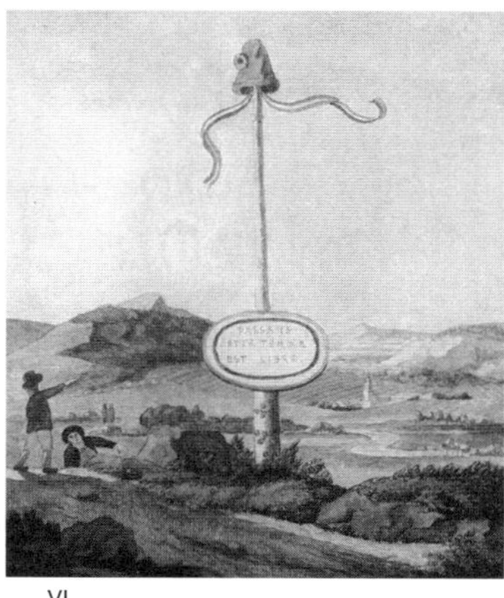

VI

IV
Jacques-Louis David, *The Death of Socrates*, 1787. Oil on canvas, 129.5 x 196.2 cm. Metropolitan Museum, New York.

V
Édouard Manet, *Ragpicker*, 1865–69. Oil on canvas, 194.9 x 130.8 cm. Norton Simon Foundation, Pasadena.

VI
Johann Wolfgang von Goethe, *Liberty Pole*, 1792. Watercolor on paper. Goethe Museum, Düsseldorf.

But the main issue here shouldn't be an artistic protection of vested rights, or the conceptual comedy of "framing or being framed." Another good subtitle, "A Conceptual Framework for Liberation," is also unfortunately already disposed of. It belongs to Gene Sharp, the pragmatic mastermind behind the politics of non-violent action, who has been given his credits recently in Tunisia and Egypt.[6] The world is full of images and it is not necessary to constantly problematize either Contextualism or de-contextualization. Sometimes problems, before they become too complicated, too abstract, too self-referential, have to be solved at a different, so-called inadequate, level and be framed from *within*: art functions in a similar way. Goethe responded to Schiller's historico-philosophical speculations in the letters *On the Aesthetic Education of Man* with his *Conversations of German Refugees*, written in a more popular style of fiction (which also, incidentally, established the novella form in German literature). Not surprisingly, we find with Goethe, too, a distanced, rather negative reaction to the French Revolution, the then current socio-political "problem" on the other side of the Rhine. The novella series' final esoteric tale, "The Fairy Tale of the Green Snake and the Beautiful Lily," through which the listener "should be reminded of nothing and everything," is an answer given in symbolic images that gently corrects the program of the letters on aesthetic education. And in this fairy tale, too, the king of wisdom is made of gold. Thomas Carlyle, who translated it into English in 1832, succeeded in using the terms "people," "crowd," and "multitude," in one single sentence. Both texts, Schiller's letters as well as Goethe's fairy tale, have, by the way, been canonical in the anthroposophic movement and Rudolf Steiner's art of education for more than a century.

There are various possibilities of reacting to revolution. One of the riskiest is to actively participate. That happened to Georg Forster in the few brief months of the short-lived Republic of Mainz —the first attempt at a democratic state in what is now Germany. (An echo of the occupation of the city by the French revolutionary troops can be found in Goethe's *Conversations*.) As representative of the Mainz Republic and President of the Jacobin club, he traveled to Paris, the capital of the revolution, at the end of March 1793 and died there of pneumonia in his attic room on rue des Moulins in January 1794, just barely forty years old. In Germany, by virtue of a decree from Emperor Francis II, which punished all collaboration by German subjects with the French revolutionary government, he was declared an outlaw and a bounty was placed on his head. Schiller

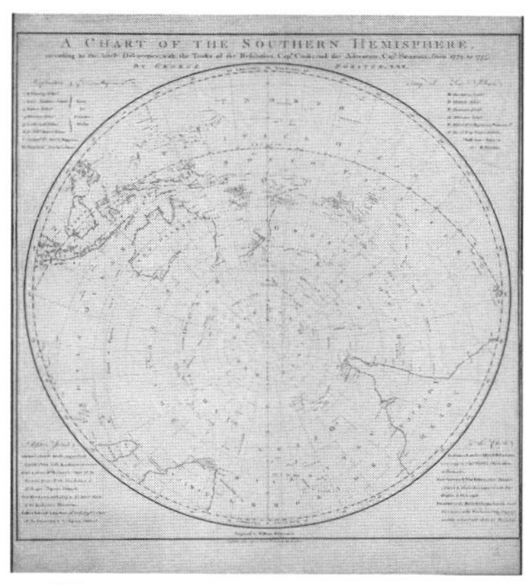

VII

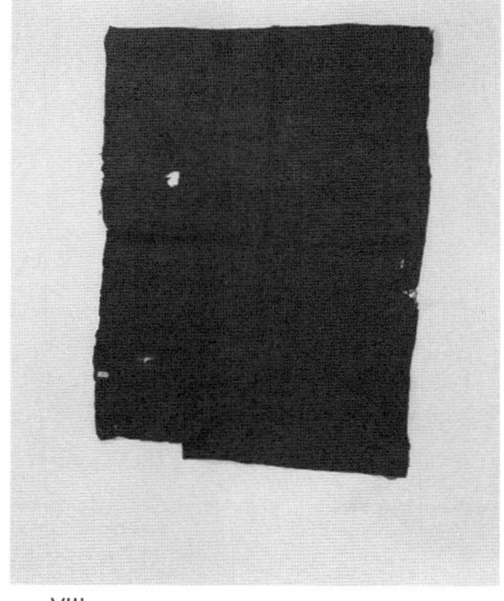

VIII

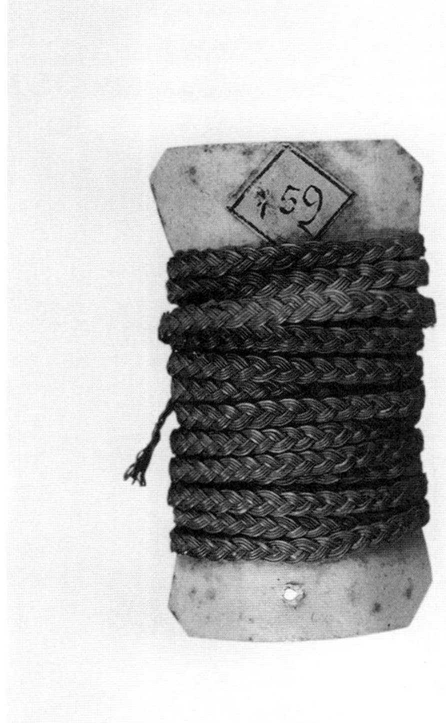

IX

VII
Map showing the southern hemisphere by Georg Forster. National Library of Australia, Canberra.

VIII
Barkcloth 'ahu, from Tahiti or the Society Islands. Cook-Forster Collection, Georg-August University, Göttingen.

IX
Cord made of coconut fibres, from the Society Islands. Cook-Forster Collection, Georg-August University, Göttingen.

X
Georg Forster,
Metrosideros umbellata,
ca. 1773. Watercolor
on paper.

XI
Georg Forster,
*Halycon leucocephala
acteon*, 1772. Water-
color on paper.

XII
Schiller's patent
of nobility. Courtesy
Austrian State
Archives, Vienna.

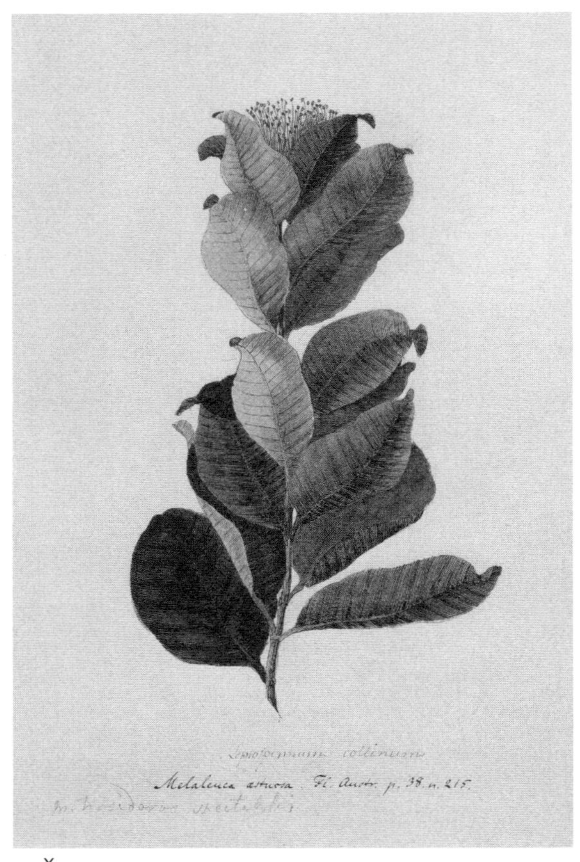

X

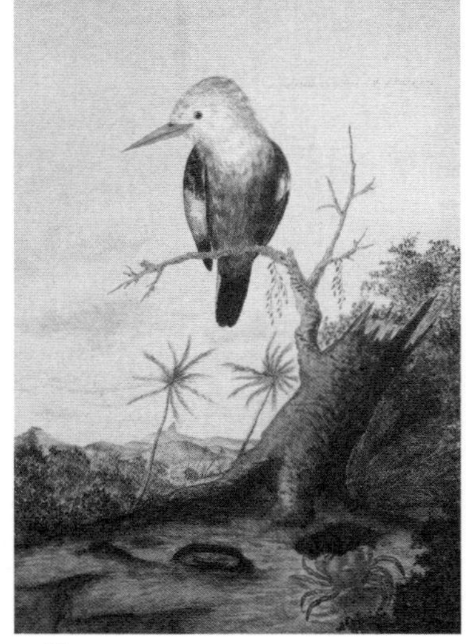

XI

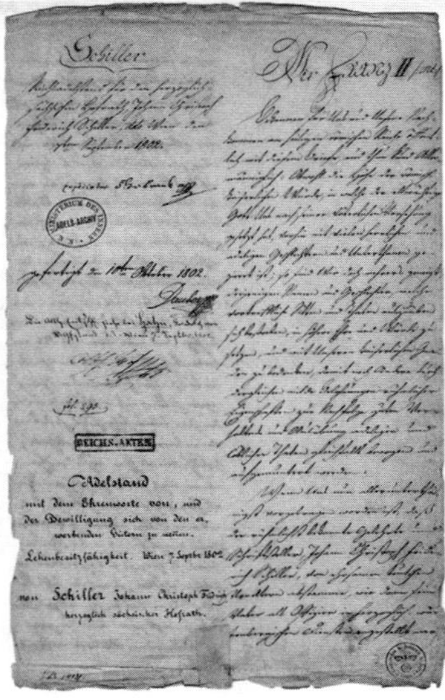

XII

and Goethe, the two major literary coalition partners, cast a few derisive distiches in his direction in their collaborative work *Xenien*.

Forster's first letter of his *Parisische Umrisse* [Parisian outlines] begins:

> France's capital has long been the haute école of insight into human nature. And it is more so now than ever before. After just a short visit and a fleeting glance one is able to fully fathom what can hardly be speculated in decades elsewhere, and to decipher not only the spirit of the present, but also the sign of the future.[7]

The author acquired this view as a traveler. At the age of seventeen he had accompanied Captain Cook on his second voyage around the world (which was meant to finally clear away the myth of *Terra australis incognita*) and made a name for himself a few years later after his return with his famous travelogue: *Cook, the Discoverer*. In it he says, "Inherent to the nature of all colonies is that as soon as they are capable of existing on their own, they emancipate themselves and tear free of their roots."[8] Catherine the Great wanted him to lead a new Pacific expedition, but the Russo-Turkish War got in the way. Accompanied by the young Alexander von Humboldt, he traveled once again through Holland, England, and France, and wrote about it. Most likely none of the German Enlightenment figures had seen as much of the world as Forster. But he was excluded from the canon of German literature as "traitor to the fatherland."

We know that Schiller never went beyond the German border his entire life; his furthest journey took him to Berlin one year before his death. But in December 1792, when the trial against Louis XVI began in Paris, he seriously considered traveling there and holding a speech at the National Assembly in defense of the king. After the king's execution in January 1793, he stopped reading French newspapers for a while. He awaited the quick demise of the Republic and refused all literary confrontations with matters of day-to-day politics. There is a certain irony in the fact that the French National Assembly named Schiller, "publiciste allemande," author of dramas, such as *The Robbers* and *Don Carlos*, an honorary citizen on 26 August 1792. The finance minister at the time, Etienne Clavière, and his colleague responsible for justice, Georges Danton, signed the document. Among the sixteen other foreign personalities honored were the German poet Klopstock, who raved about the regeneration of German letters [*Gelehrtenrepublik*], two pedagogues—Joachim Heinrich Campe and Johann Heinrich Pestalozzi —George Washington, Jeremy Bentham (who called the *Declaration of Men and of the Citizen* "nonsense upon stilts" and at the time was already busy with his panopticon prison of total surveillance), as well as Joseph Priestley who isolated the element oxygen. Among them, too, was the eccentric Anacharsis Cloots, "orator of mankind" and "a personal enemy of God." He came from Kleve on the Lower Rhine, as did Joseph Beuys, who honored him as the first to "develop a genuine theory of democracy." All told, it was an obstinate mixture that had been thought out there in Paris.

Thanks to Lacan we know that a letter always reaches its destination. Yet due to the political situation in those years, the honorary diploma didn't reach the addressee until 1798, six years later. Of those who had issued it, not a single one was still alive. In 1802, Schiller was elevated to nobility by Emperor Francis II.

Concepts and forms travel, too. Or should we speak about migration instead? The refugee is the avant-garde, but there is no heaven for concepts. The rhetoric in Schiller's letters, equally suggestive and open, which has as much as survived all interpretation, ends as is well known with the question of whether and where "such a State of Beauty in Appearance," that is, the aesthetic State, can be found. "As a need, it exists in every finely tuned soul; as an achievement we might perhaps find it ... only in a few select circles...."[9] Yes, for example, at the Duke's court in Weimar, one is immediately tempted to add. Accusations of compensation were maintained for quite some time in the Marxist reception of the letters. But Schiller's ideas—that's the most fascinating thing about their form—are good for the most contrary projections. The "play drive" that Schiller introduced in the fourteenth letter, in order to "aim at the extinction of time in time,"[10] also haunts the history of so-called progressive education, that is, from Schiller's contemporary Pestalozzi through to Friedrich Fröbel's *The Education of Man* and the kindergarten movement to Maria Montessori and Célestin Freinet. And aren't children the true subalterns? How subversive is the history of childhood? On the eve of World War II, Johan Huizinga created "Homo Ludens," which in the post-war era became an often-quoted and increasingly safe term of consensus of modernity.

At this point I would like to briefly recall a painter's attempt to write a "Reconstruction of philosophy from the standpoint of an artist." I am referring to Asger Jorn, co-founder of CoBrA and the Situationist International. Before that, he was also a communist resistance fighter during the Nazi occupation of Denmark. He had quickly noticed that painting wasn't going to work against the Nazis. Lying in the sanatorium in Silkeborg with tuberculosis in 1952, he wrote *Held og Hasard: Dolk og Guitar* [*Luck and Chance: Dagger and Guitar*]. In the chapter "Aesthetics as amusement or diversion," he states: "Schiller defined aesthetics as play, from which it follows that the aesthetician is the player."[11] Jorn submitted his unorthodox thesis as a doctoral dissertation, but it was rejected by a philosophy professor at the University of Copenhagen.

Does anyone here remember Herbert Marcuse, the German immigrant and philosopher who became a pop icon in California and worldwide at the age of seventy? His book *Eros and Civilization*, written in the early 1950s at the height of the McCarthy era, was a socio-political draft for emancipation, which attempted to combine Marx with Freud (whereby Marx is not mentioned by name in the book). It was emphatically and hedonistically taken up by the 1960s protest movements. The third in the trio is Friedrich Schiller, with his letters on the aesthetic education of man. In the chapter "The Aesthetic Dimension," Schiller is made chief witness and mentor of a revolutionary cultural transformation. Marcuse opposes the capitalist order's repressive performance principle with his "logic of gratification," in which Eros and sensuousness are antidotes to a logic of production based on the division of labor: "The aesthetic form is sensuous form—constituted by the *order of sensuousness*."[12] Schiller's play drive was enthroned as an emancipatory impulse with subversive intentions. Also the "conquest of time in so far as time is destructive of lasting gratification" is a part of this program.[13] Marcuse spoke of the "explosive quality of Schiller's conception" and without any reservations or philological scruples declared it a contemporary political program. Never before, and never again, has Schiller's ambivalent metaphor of the aesthetic state been taken as literally as in Marcuse's optimistic interpretation. The age of access — with time as the ultimate resource — was still very much in the future.

There is no clear answer to the question of how artists should respond to revolution. In the early 1970s, this was also T.J. Clark's art-historical conclusion on the Courbet case: "It seems to be an opportunity, and for those like Courbet who seize it, it seems to be intrinsic to their greatest work."[14] But that already no longer applied to Courbet's successors, who were working off realism similar to the way that contemporary art is working off context. The strange thing about a neo-Impressionist painting, such as *Il Quarto Stato* [*The Fourth Estate*] by Giuseppe Pellizza da Volpedo, completed after years of torment in 1901, is perhaps precisely the excessive

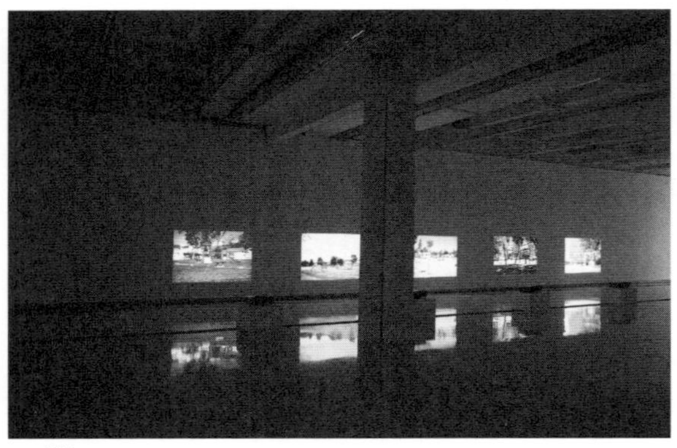

XIII

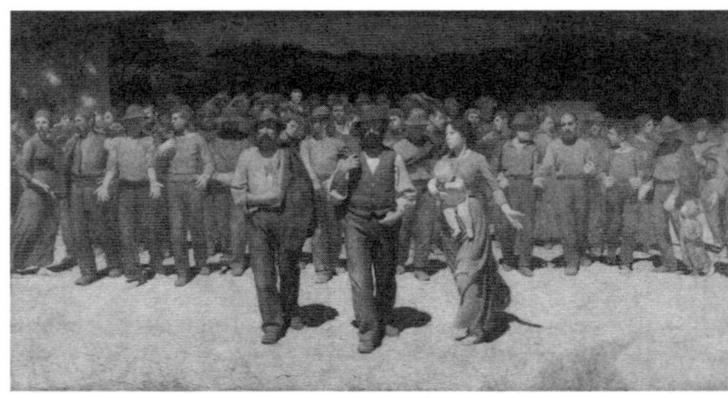

XIV

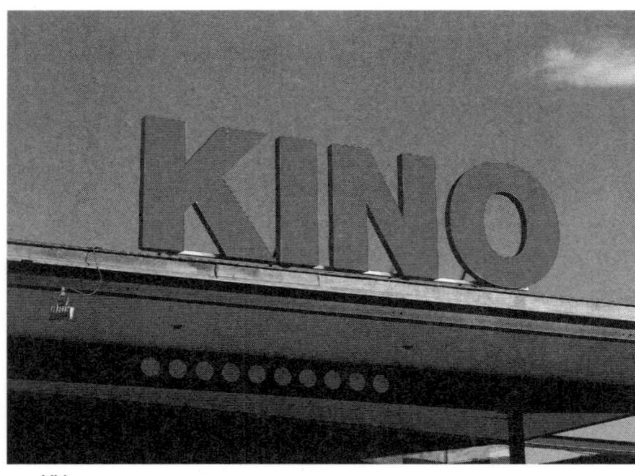

XV

XIII
Peter Friedl, *Playgrounds*, 1995–2010. Digitized slides, five wall projections. Installation view: Sala Rekalde, Bilbao. Courtesy the artist. (Photo: Begoña Zubero)

XIV
Giuseppe Pellizza da Volpedo, *Il Quarto Stato*, 1901. Oil on canvas, 293 x 545 cm. Museo del Novecento, Milan.

XV
Peter Friedl, *KINO*, 1997. Documenta X, Kassel. Courtesy the artist and Vanhaerents Art Collection, Brussels. (Photo: Dieter Schwerdtle).

self-indulgence with which it presents itself to a secular contingency, and not only because of the obvious reference to Raphael's *School of Athens*. The world of the twentieth century was panoramic. The artist's suicide by hanging—in the studio, in front of precisely this wide screen portrait of the working class—transformed his painting into cinema. It was the era of Puccini's greatest opera triumphs.

Perhaps it is one of the privileges of being an emeritus professor to take things into one's own hands and enjoy them. Just what is it that makes today's art world so different, so appealing? The symbiotic relationship between a philosopher and the art world —or more precisely: between a philosopher and that part of the art world that is interested in and profiting from discursive surplus value —follows genre-specific dramaturgical rules. The curatorial regime tightly anchored in today's art world functions essentially through uncontested exclusion and forgetfulness. It thereby organizes distribution and visibility at various social levels—for example, those of information, promotion, and canonization. The bizarre career of the curator within one generation—from arranger to auteur without a work—can best be understood as a coup. (Consequently, art critique has also been eliminated.) "A force is a force," it says in *The Ignorant Schoolmaster*.[15] Power is power. It meanders through all levels, even through us, because it is never just elsewhere, and as we know (I am flirting with a text of mine, from 2000, a little travelogue manifesto about Haiti and concept art), power can only be practiced through the production of truth.[16] Power is based on agreement and consensus.

Everything is in everything. In the real aesthetic of hyper-capitalism, "contemporary art" functions like a brand name whereby it remains largely unclear what the brand is. But that is how this new order and its global market work. The term "resistance" is either naïve or a simple marketing concept, except when one truly says "no," and acts on it. Aesthetic resistance is a rather lonely business. In a statement on the occasion of a meeting of international museum people some ten years ago, I made the following suggestion:

> Museums are never autonomous and neither are artworks.
> Also questionable is the oft-evoked autonomy of market
> forces. What does exist, however, is aesthetic autonomy
> as a concept and as a direct experience… [The artist's
> autonomy] expresses itself in the freedom of being able to say
> no from time to time when nothing better comes to mind.[17]

That looks like an emergency program for post-democracy, but could just as well be "aesthetic education" (or, self-education) and intellectual emancipation. Their forms and methods are more fragile than one would like them to be. And fragility is a strange thing to discuss.

Every intelligent, non-hierarchical approach that believes in an ethics of cooperation and simultaneously accepts the criteria or principles of the curatorial regime as given, tends to further consolidate and co-manage it. It is then mainly "motifs" that are created, offered, and gratefully picked up on—a favorite occupation of many actors in the art world. The philosopher ("I always try to think in terms of horizontal distributions"[18]) hereby becomes a co-curator. One could also somewhat maliciously call that the "bureaucratic" collateral damage of the above-mentioned symbiotic relationship. It seems a bit strange when dealing with ideas aiming at political and aesthetic dissent. But perhaps the philosopher's political ideas also already work more like motifs.

It seems to me that a whole series of important questions and problems do not get their fair share in all of that. Among them, to stay with my métier, is the exhibition as a "medium"—as the site of a public staging where art spins its own web; where images are experienced as the production of a narrative rather than as the illustration of an already existing narrative. That would mean that there is a commitment to make accessible the creative potential of images, rather than to subjugate them to the discourse carried on about them. All images lie when they are not read right. I argue for more critical intimacy. The operational conundrum of how something can be framed from within has already been addressed.

To cite and denounce another concrete deficiency: the scandalous impasse and formal routine afflicting contemporary exhibition display. Art is usually presented as though it were exclusively about products by artists; context is reduced to text. Another problem is the particular *temporality* of artworks, that is, their relative autonomy or solitude in the netherland between production and reception (often also called "understanding"). Artworks do not have to be understood immediately and directly. They can be their own discourses and analyses: immanent scenarios of aesthetic experience. Some of them perhaps do not even need us in our function as beholder and participant.

Where and how such things can be taught and learned is another issue. In other words: institutions should learn how to dramatize their identity problems *formally* more convincingly than they normally do. Instead of preaching re-education, they would do better to transform themselves unconditionally, like in a fairy tale. We're talking about an effort and aesthetic intelligence that goes beyond the regulated playground.

1 Jacques Rancière, *The Politics of Aesthetics: The Distribution of the Sensible*, trans. Gabriel Rockhill (London and New York: Continuum, 2004), 86.

2 See Jean-Luc Godard interviewed by Jean-Marc Lalanne, "Le droit d'auteur? Un auteur n'a que des devoirs," *Les Inrockuptibles*, 18 May 2010. Retrieved from http://blogs.lesinrocks.com/cannes2010/2010/05/18/le-droit-dauteur-un-auteur-na-que-des-devoirs-jean-luc-godard/

3 Ibid.

4 Giorgio Agamben, *The Man Without Content*, trans. Georgia Albert (Stanford, CA: Standford University Press, 1999). For inexplicable reasons, in the American edition there's a note stating: "*The Man Without Content* was originally published in Italian in 1994 as *L'uomo senza contenuto*." The first Italian edition was published in 1970.

5 See Frank Wagner, "Fragen an Jeff Wall," in *Jeff Wall, Szenarien im Bildraum der Wirklichkeit: Essays und Interviews*, ed. Gregor Stemmrich (Dresden: Verlag der Kunst, 1997), 334.

6 Gene Sharp, *From Dictatorship to Democracy: A Conceptual Framework for Liberation* (Boston: The Albert Einstein Institution, 2002).

7 "Die Hauptstadt Frankreichs war seit langer Zeit die hohe Schule der Menschenkenntniß. Mehr als jemals ist sie es jetzt, und es bedarf nur eines kurzen Aufenathalts und eines flüchtigen Blicks, um hier inne zu werden, was man anderwärts in Jahrzehenden kaum ergrübelt, und nicht nur den Geist der Gegenwart, sondern auch die Zeichen der Zukunft zu enträthseln." Georg Forster, "Parisische Umrisse," in Georg Forster, *Ausgewählte Schriften* (Warendorf: Verlag Johannes G. Hoof, 2003), 364.

8 "Die Naturen aller Kolonien bringt es mit sich, daß sie, sobald sie für sich selbst bestehen können, sich emancipiren und vom alten Stamme losreißen." Georg Forster, "Cook, der Entdecker," in *Ausgewählte Schriften*, p. 153. The South Seas expedition was commissioned by the London Royal Society; Georg Forster was officially employed as a "draughtsman." Most of the numerous objects collected by him and his father, Reinhold Forster, on their journey, are in the Cook-Forster Collection in Göttingen.

9 Friedrich Schiller, *On the Aesthetic Education of Man*, trans. Reginald Snell (Mineola, NY: Dover, 2004), 140.

10 Ibid., 74.

11 See Asger Jorn, *The Natural Order and Other Texts*, trans. Peter Shield (Burlington, VT: Ashgate, 2002). Retrieved from http://dysphasiapress.org/luckand-chance.html#diversion

12 Herbert Marcuse, *Eros and Civilization: A Philosophical Inquiry into Freud* (Abingdon: Routledge & Kegan, 1998), 185.

13 Ibid., p. 193.

14 T.J. Clark, *The Absolute Bourgeois: Artists and Politics in France 1848–1851* (London: Thames and Hudson, 1973), 182.

15 Jacques Rancière, *The Ignorant Schoolmaster: Five Lessons in Intellectual Emancipation*, trans. Kristin Ross (Stanford, CA: Stanford University Press, 1991), 91.

16 See Peter Friedl, "The Curse of the Iguana: On Genre and Power," in *Peter Friedl, Secret Modernity: Selected Writings and Interviews 1981–2009*, trans. Lisa Rosenblatt (Berlin and New York: Sternberg, 2010), 138.

17 Peter Friedl, "One World," in *Secret Modernity*, 166.

18 Rancière, *The Politics of Aesthetics*, 49.

4

COMMUNIST EDUCATION

Jan Voelker

I have to start with a deviation from our subject. Some months ago many of us were following as closely as we could the riots in the Arab countries. The events taking place in Tahrir square and elsewhere opened up a new possibility for politics. A feeling of sympathy, close to enthusiasm, arose in us for the strength and the simplicity of this "will of the people," as Peter Hallward would call it,[1] gathering itself there with the sole aim of emancipation. The absence of any radical Islamist ideology was so blatantly apparent that even Western politicians had to refrain at one point from their instant first reaction, which was to warn us about the danger of instability and the possibility of an Islamist takeover. Indeed, the opposite was happening: it was precisely the absence of any fundamentalist religious speech as well as the absence of any call for Western democracy that were among the decisive characteristics of the protests.

And then we had to admit: that this was never thought to be possible. Did we not all implicitly believe the common myth that the people in these countries were not really able to emancipate themselves, but rather could only fall prey to radical Islamism at some point? At least we allowed ourselves to be told by our media and our contemporaries that due to the lack of enlightenment, emancipatory movements would have no chance in the Middle East.

We have been taught the opposite. We have been taught that we have to mistrust our conception of the possible and that we should instead develop our concept of the impossible. What we should learn is that we know nothing about the impossible. We not only know nothing, but we take this lack of knowledge as a lack of existence. And we take it as a barrier for our thought: we literally try to think only within the constraints of our knowledge.

And if it were only for polemical reasons, to begin to learn, to be taught by the impossible, we should remind ourselves that the strongest barrier of impossibility is now on our side: it is in fact impossible to have political uprisings in our secure first world. So there are two faces of the impossible. On the one side it functions as a prohibition, and on the other side it seems that what is new finds its starting point outside of the realm of our knowledge.

We can assert that it is a fact that for us today politics has become impossible. Politics in the precise sense of the embodying of a new process of emancipation that would be beyond our knowledge of the techniques of society. Without having the space to further elaborate this point, we can cite the name Alain Badiou, who has obviously worked on this knot with the utmost precision.[2]

What we should learn then is that, from the impossible, politics itself can take form. If one supposes that we could learn this from the events in the Middle East, then a fundamental question has to be answered: in what way and to what extent do these events relate to us, to our situation? To this question there is a first, quite common answer. A stupid answer: namely, another question about the continuation of the oil supplies from Libya or bringing up the threat of refugees heading towards European soil. A German newspaper put it the following way: if Saudi Arabia also has its riots, oil prices would be affected dramatically, and then the Arab Spring would finally arrive in Europe—at gas stations.

But the real question is indeed, how do we and how can we relate to the impossible events we witnessed? How can we learn more about the question of the impossible? To say it differently, and to put it as Alain Badiou has put it recently, we should be pupils of these movements. But how can we be pupils of foreign events?[3]

This whole question might be understood as a deviation away from the subject of aesthetic education. But my point will be, as you might guess, that on the contrary this is not a deviation at all, and that we can connect these problems if we look into Rancière's works on aesthetics, and try to elaborate and extend his argument as to what it means to follow an emancipatory lesson today.

So the first part of the question could be put the following way: is it possible to learn from emancipatory movements? Is something like an emancipatory education possible? To say the least, one would at first say that this is very problematic. We might end up placing the emancipatory movement in the position of some kind of master, and the emancipatory education would, in its educational part, not be emancipatory at all. We cannot be the pupils of these events in the sense that there is some sort of a master-image telling us how emancipation would work not only in this particular instance, but in general. A second argument might state that we simply cannot learn anything from any other moment of emancipation, because the situation is completely different, due to different cultures, etc. But clearly, these arguments would not be universalist enough. The universalist stance would rather be that those events, as events of emancipation, in their truth address anybody, anybody who is willing to engage himself in the emancipatory process; they are neither a master plan for other situations nor is the conception of equality they propose different than any other situation. So, one has to stick to the question and even generalize it: is there any possibility of emancipatory education at all?

With Rancière, one has to think emancipation in terms of time and space, and therefore the relation between art and politics, which lies at the heart of Rancière's thought. And in relation to the question of how to learn from emancipatory moments, the question of art will come to be decisive. This would then be the second part of the question: can we frame a certain thought of emancipatory education within the constellation of politics and art that Rancière claims to be central for the aesthetic regime?

The scene of emancipation, or:
How to pass from one to the other

Let us start with the role of education in the process of emancipation. In a recent book, *The Emancipated Spectator*,[4] Rancière has taken up the thread of education again, which he had opened at a very early point of his thought. He reminds us of the ignorant schoolmaster Jacotot, to whom Rancière dedicated a book,[5] and he reminds us of the scene of emancipation that was to be found in Jacotot's system of education. The system that Jacotot developed was based on the interruption of the classical scene of education in which a knowing master and an unknowing pupil form the central constellation. In *The Emancipated Spectator*, Rancière transforms this constellation into the constellation we find in a theatre, namely the constellation of a group of spectators before a performance.

As in his book on Jacotot, where Rancière undermines the relation between the active and the passive, the knowing school-master and the unknowing pupil or the *ignoramus*, Rancière's aim is to change our fundamental conception of the relation between the audience and the work of art. He does not attempt to turn the audience into an active, interacting audience that would be integrated in the performance. Rather one has to interrupt the relation of the master and the pupil at its very roots: Rancière's attempt is—as Jacotot showed—to understand the spectator as someone who already has a certain knowledge. With the help of this knowledge which anybody already has at his or her disposal, this anybody is capable of working on his own sense of the spectacle, of creating his or her own sense out of it. Because this power of translation is the capacity of anyone, the community in play is the community of anybodies, unspecified, gathered together only in their commonly shared capacity to translate.

In turn, the artist, Rancière adds, is not a person transforming his knowledge or his ideas via the medium of the artwork, then placing it into the realm of the spectator: he or she is instead working on the transformation of something he or she does not know into an artwork. So the artist, too, is involved in a process of translation. He is transferring his knowledge into a scene where he is also a spectator and does not know what actually is taking place. The artist makes himself a spectator, while the spectator makes himself a translator, a narrator, or, in short: an artist.

Indeed, Rancière reproduces the scene of Jacotot here. In the book on Jacotot, the teacher becomes an ignorant teacher, and the pupil becomes someone who already has knowledge, and they both come together in a shared absence of a specific knowledge. In the exemplary case of Jacotot, both the teacher and pupil do not speak the language of the other, and so neither one can instruct the other. They cannot communicate. Jacotot had to go into exile, and now he does not know how to continue teaching, since he is not able to communicate with his pupils. But what he does have is a book. In Jacotot's case, it is a copy of Fénelon's *The Adventures of Telemachus*, a bilingual edition with the original text and a translation on facing pages. Not only there is a translation of the French into Flemish; this book is also a translation of a classical text into modernity, so it is really a translation machine. This changes the situation of education. Because now both sides find proof that translation is possible, and word-by-word they can start their own translation and learn the language of the other, without any instruction or explanation. With only a bit of knowledge at their disposal they are able to translate the book: because "everything is in everything"[6] and "*all men have equal intelligence*"[7]—anybody is able to connect the knowledge he has to new knowledge.

Rancière calls the "normal" situation of education the situation of inequality because it rests on the distinction between the knowing and the unknowing. The situation of emancipation, however, is the situation of equality, because it is free of any determination and it is through learning that both persons will prove that their knowledge is equally capable of learning the language of the other. They proceed from the knowledge they have and learn by themselves. Nevertheless one has to remember the fact that the emancipatory scene is still a scene of education, and the schoolmaster is an ignorant one, but still a schoolmaster. Rancière's (and Jacotot's) objection is directed against the transmission of knowledge from a knowing person to an unknowing. It is *this* hierarchy that is abolished in the emancipatory scene. But what is still transmitted, even and perhaps most necessarily in the emancipatory scene, is the will. The schoolmaster is able to encourage the will of the other, to make him want to translate. This will is transmitted via the book; this transmission between the two unknowing persons is only possible via the book as a medium.

If we come back to the scene of art, and its relation between an artist and an audience, there is obviously only one candidate left to take the role of the book: the work of art itself. The work of art becomes a kind of third, a mediation between the artist and the spectator. But this middle term does not mediate a specific content. It is an empty place, just as Jacotot's book is an empty third. Empty in the precise sense that the confrontation between two languages does not exhibit the process of translation; the bilingual book is only a material effect that proves the possibility of a process of translation retroactively.

The problem with this scene of emancipation, as Rancière has several times stated it in relation to Jacotot, is that it does not lead us to any political scene. For Jacotot, emancipation is always possible, but it is always the emancipation of the individual. Nothing leads from individual emancipation to an emancipated society, because the latter is necessarily always structured and hierarchical. In his book *Disagreement,* Rancière therefore shifts the argument: If Jacotot's claim was that emancipation will always be lost as soon as an attempt is made to integrate it into the social order of bodies and spaces, Rancière now starts from the axiom that the social order of bodies and spaces inscribes a "wrong" into society, that is, it mistreats equality. Emancipation can then be thought at the level of communities, because now society establishes scenes of inequality and produces an unspecified, uncounted remainder. This remainder is *per se* collective. Rancière thus shifts the problem of emancipation from an individual to a collective level.

So emancipatory education seems to encounter a problem, as soon as it translated into the context of a collective. Already in Jacotot's practice, we seem at some point to lose the idea of the collective or of the community. Clearly, the question of community is also part of the classical scene of education: for it is obvious that if a

teacher transmits knowledge to the brains of his pupils, he might be able to build up a sort of a perverted collective, in which everyone knows the same thing in the end. For as long as it has existed, the classical scene of education has been about the reproduction of the state.

In the scene of emancipation, then, this social link is lost. This is indeed not a side effect; the loss of the social link is rather one of the central moments of the emancipation. The emancipatory process consists primarily of a practice of dis-identification: don't be a knowing teacher anymore, don't be an unknowing pupil anymore. Emancipation is the loss of roles and places. Jacotot seems to leave us with a mass of emancipated individuals, and it is not clear how to make the way to a political collective from here. Jacotot simply escapes this question by claiming that emancipation cannot rise to the level of society. Impossible.

But even in the emancipatory scene, there are always two. In the scene of emancipation no knowledge will be transmitted, but there is a will to be passed on. You always need the ignorant schoolmaster to encourage the will of the other. To put it differently, looking from the other side, from the side of the one who is seeking knowledge: what you need is not a master, what you need is not only the will to translate and to learn, but also the courage for the new. It is the ignorant schoolmaster who encourages, but the book does as well, as a manifest example that the impossible already has been possible. The schoolmaster can transmit his will, and the book is a material proof of possible emancipation.

Courage, which we can add as a supplement to the Rancièrian framework, can be taken from a famous phrase of Kant that could perhaps serve as a motto for Jacotot's scene of emancipation. "Have courage to make use of your *own* understanding!" was Kant's well-known answer to the question: What is Enlightenment?[8] In this sense, the needed courage is the courage for the new, supplementing the will for new knowledge. So will and courage, in a way, form the link between the emancipated schoolmaster, the pupil who is about to emancipate himself, and the book. But this will is still not a collective will. It is, if one may put it like this, the will of the two.

Now, if we think of a group of pupils, say, it is still unclear if this will also allows us to connect people in an emancipatory moment. We could say that at the heart of the question of education there persists the question of the translation of a dis-identifying and dissociating method into a political collective. Given that this is also the problem of the transition from Jacotot's emancipatory scene to a scene of collectivization, I would propose to call it the problem of communist education.

To elaborate this problem, we can change our perspective. In a talk Rancière gave at the first conference on the *Idea of Communism* in May 2009 in London, he addressed this problem again. He asked: "The question is: how can the collectivization of the capacity of anybody coincide with the global organization of a society? How can the anarchical principle of emancipation become the principle of a social distribution of tasks, positions and powers?"[9] In associating himself with the Badiou's *Communist Hypothesis*, Rancière claims that we need a sort of history of communist moments, which we can soon understand as moments of emancipation. This history would rather be a non-history of moments in which ordinary time is interrupted, a non-history of singular points of timelessness.[10]

Emancipation is always un-timely, being precisely a split within time and space. And if we want to think emancipation in a collective framework—what Rancière here, and I would say after a long time, calls Communism again—we would have to disentangle these communist moments from the narratives that try to join them to a story with a necessity and an inner goal. At the level of structure, we confront the same problem here: how to unite moments of dis-identification? Rancière's answer seems in part to be that the rethinking of communist moments as they have existed may encourage us or give us "confidence"[11] in the possibility of the impossible. They give us the confidence to think the impossible because they are themselves a collection of impossibilities that happened in space and time. Now, why does Rancière speak of Communism here? He gives three reasons, which I will briefly quote: the first is that the name communism "emphasizes the principle of the unity and equality of intelligences"; the second is that "it emphasizes the affirmative aspect of the process of collectivization of this principle"; and finally "it stresses the self-superseding capacity of the process, its boundlessness, which entails its ability to invent futures that are not yet imaginable."[12]

The aspects of affirmation and the superseding quality of the process are in a certain sense relatively new in Rancière's conception of the process of emancipation. One could relate them back to the scene of emancipation and to its notion of the encouragement needed for the process of emancipation to take place. "Communism" names the type of link that was earlier found between the will and courage, that is, a link of indetermination. But in this linking of different scenes of collective emancipation, in this linking of communist moments of the past to those of the future, it is also already collective structures that are linked. If we speak of courage, if we speak of confidence, or the will, we can now speak about a collective courage or collective confidence. We are in the realm of what in a political sense we can call communist education, in the sense Rancière gives to the word: emphasizing the unity and equality of intelligences, the affirmative aspect of the process of collectivization, and the inner boundlessness of this process. Communist education turns the scene of emancipation into a collective one: but a collective scene of confidence and courage for emancipation, not a collective that would in any sense be determined.

So we gain confidence from past moments. But the problem of education also refers us to the question as to how we can be taught by events actually happening in the present? For the time being, we have only transferred the scene of emancipation from an individual level to a collective one, but we still do not see very clearly how the process of collectivization could arise.

I think that we can find in Rancière a very special proposition in which we are taught to be confident not only historically, but in the present. This proposition also concerns the question how this confidence can be built, and where it can stem from, in those times in which collective emancipation is absent. And, despite all the parallels, I think on this point the art object shows itself to be, for Rancière, a different kind of object than Jacotot's book was.

The Scene of Art

At the beginning I claimed that if we really want ask how we can learn from emancipatory moments in Rancière, then we would have to ask about art. And after this detour concerning the question of how the individual scene of emancipation can be turned into a collective one, determining the link without a link that courage is, and showing how this courage may be won historically, we can now finally turn to art. The first question is simple and obvious. If what I would like to call—for reasons that will soon be explained—*the scene of art* reproduces the scene of emancipation as witnessed in Jacotot, do we not encounter once again the problem that the scene of art is not a political scene and there is no path that leads from the scene of art to a political scene? As we have seen, Rancière draws parallels between the scene of art and Jacotot's scene of emancipation, and we actually do encounter the same problem here. But with a slight change indeed, because now the question is rather how to get from the scene of an object (of art) to a subjective process. It is not about emancipation as a process between two individuals anymore, but about emancipation as a subjective process in relation to a specific object. Still, one could say that this closely resembles the scene of emancipation and the importance of the book in it. But the role of the book in Jacotot and the role of work of art function differently, and I will try to explain why.

In his book *The Emancipated Spectator*, Rancière asserts that "Emancipation begins when we challenge the opposition between viewing and acting; when we understand that the self-evident facts that structure the relations between saying, seeing and doing themselves belong to the structure of domination and subjection,"[13] and this definition is meant to define the disruptive effect of artworks, though we could also relate it to Jacotot.

In the book cited, Rancière is speaking about works of art, mostly theatrical performances. Such performances, like any other art work belonging to the realm of the aesthetic regime, can be characterized following Rancière as something producing sensory anomalies, disrupting the orders of time and space, dissociating the chain of cause and effect. In this way, art objects or scenes of art produce an effect of disruption. And with regard to the spectator they produce a dis-identification, and even a "community of dis-identifed persons."[14] Artworks neither represent emancipation nor do they immediately incorporate it. They are some kind of third, like Jacotot's book, and they can be a tool of emancipation.

Now it is here that one encounters several problems. First, it is clear that Rancière conceives of artworks as related to emancipation. But it is far from obvious how to understand this relation when we have to understand emancipation as something more than Jacotot did, as more than individual emancipation.

The first thing we can observe is that both the book in Jacotot's emancipatory scene and the work of art occupy the place of the object. There are individuals who emancipate themselves in relation to a certain object. Emancipation itself can never be objectified, it can never be caught in determinations and definitions, it is a purely subjective process, but it is a process in relation to objects or to objectivity. The object itself cannot be emancipatory: we cannot say that Jacotot's book in itself is emancipatory, or possesses some strange emancipatory energy. Neither can we say anything similar about the work of art. But it does have a certain political effect. It has, as Rancière puts it, "a political effect to the extent that the loss of destination it presupposes disrupts the way in which bodies fit their functions and destinations."[15] This is where the aesthetic and the political intersect, at the site of the disruptive effect.

But let us stay with the object for a moment. The work of art disrupts the normal order of the sensible, and the political procedure finds its starting point in such a rupture. This disrupting of the normal order of space and time is a negative effect of the work of art. It is its de-specification, its not-fitting-in, its withdrawing from the structure of distinction, its undecidability as an object that makes it a strange, alien object in time and space. As an object in time and space, the art object claims to be itself another, general order of space and time in the same moment it continues to remain an alien object within the normal order of space and time. This other space and time, which it is, even as it remains inside the same, normal space and time—because the work of art disrupts the order of the sensible as a sensible being itself—can therefore only be a split. It is a split in the order of space and time in the precise sense of being both: out of and in this world. It is in this world, made out of it, and outside of it.

What is the object that is called an art object, then? We are left with two possibilities: either we understand objects of art to be those objects that are singular ruptures in the sensible, or we assert that this split in the sensible can be encountered anywhere, and everything can possibly be a work of art. The second answer resembles the Deleuzian one, in the sense of an event that would be integrated into the univocity of being. Rancière's answer seems to be the first one, emphasizing that objects of art objectify ruptures of the sensible in the form of produced objects.

If we now move to the side of the spectator, we encounter the same question: either we conceive of the spectator as dependent on the concrete object in his process of emancipation, or we understand the spectator as fully independent of the object. If he or she were dependent on the object of art in the process of emancipation, we would have to assume that art objects are in the position of mastery in the process of emancipation. Only artworks would be able to initiate the process of emancipation in the spectator. If we strengthen this position a bit further, we could say that this position resembles the aesthetics of the sublime, insofar as only the art object would have the power to produce a disruptive shock. And, on the other side: if he or she were fully independent, we would completely lose the connection to the works of art. For Rancière, as I would like to put it, the spectator is not independent, for it is in the process of emancipation that he establishes a link of indetermination in relation to the work of art.

What the spectator has to do, then, is translate the process inherent in the work of art into his own emancipation. But this process is a process of dis-identification. It is a process of dis-identification and a process of learning that the impossible is possible, that it is possible to do what one cannot do. To speak another language in the case of Jacotot, or create different orders of the sensible in the case of works of art—both are scenes of emancipation. As in the scene of emancipation in Jacotot, we learn from the scene of art to deploy our own (non-teleological) will, and we learn that we have the capacity to learn and do what we will. As with Jacotot's book, the work of art does not teach us any knowledge, but rather teaches us a confidence in the impossible. This confidence has then to be turned into a knowledge again, because we do not speak any language based on confidence alone. What the object really teaches us is the confidence to turn the impossible into the possible.

The object of art, however, teaches in a different way than Jacotot's book. In contrast to the scene of emancipation, the scene of art contains a certain collective dimension, but in contrast to a political scene, the scene of art is not yet fully collectivized.

Take the way Rancière speaks about the process of emancipation in relation to the spectators:

> The collective power shared by spectators does not stem
> from the fact that they are members of a collective body
> or from some specific form of interactivity. It is the power
> each of them has to translate what she perceives in her
> own way, to link it to the unique intellectual adventure
> that makes her similar to all the rest in as much as this
> adventure is not like any other.[16]

It is a shared effect of disruption that forms the aesthetic community, we could say. So here the aesthetic community is formed through the collective experience of a singular situation of dis-identification. But, as Rancière does not wait to add, from this kind of intellectual awareness there is no road that leads to a political community. Again, there is no path from an aesthetic emancipation to a political scene. But if we return to the moment of confidence which Rancière described in relation to the communist moments, could we not say that works of art can give us confidence that a different order of the sensible is possible? And could we not say that this confidence is in itself only possible as a collective effect, precisely because the art scene is not an individual scene, but a scene that we could call public? It is public because it is in space and time, and because it directly refers to space and time. If the book is a translation machine, the scene of art is a direct intervention in space and time. And, publicly, it immanently addresses everyone. This is also why art objects actually form scenes of art, because they are always necessarily integrated in a space and a time, and as a split in space and time they depend on a public "audience." Otherwise the intervention in space and time through the art object would not be real.

The universal address via the medium of an object is what the spectators witness. A universal address, because it is a singular object in space and time, and as such it addresses potentially everyone. Ruptures in space and time are totalizing: they are perhaps minimal points, but they claim to be a totality. They are and they claim to be objective. So there is an address to everyone, but this address is only a negative one, because the art object is only a rupture in space and time that shows the spectator negatively that there is a distribution of space and time that does not relate to us all and that there are other possible distributions, and that therefore the possibility of other distributions will bring a founding equality to light. And therefore equality is always there and will always already have been there. But: what is this addressing of everyone in the singular distribution like? How can it touch us, if we are not able to see it, because this rupture is in itself nothing, being only a material effect in space and time?

There is a famous passage in Kant's *Conflict of the Faculties* that is very similar to Rancière's claim about the spectator, although he himself does not mention it. Kant is writing about the French Revolution, and for him it is essentially the spectator of the event who is the important figure. Kant writes that

> The revolution that we have seen taking place in our own
> times in a nation of gifted people may succeed, or it may
> fail. It may be so filled with misery and atrocities that no
> right-thinking man would ever decide to make the same
> experiment again at such price, even if he could hope to
> carry it out successfully at the second attempt. But I main-
> tain that this revolution has aroused in the hearts and desires
> of all spectators who are not themselves caught up in it a
> sympathy that borders almost on enthusiasm, although the
> very utterance of this sympathy was fraught with danger. It
> cannot therefore have been caused by anything other than a
> moral disposition within the human race.[17]

Instead of reading here an indication of a tendency towards morality in mankind, one can also understand this differently. At this point we should take up an argument that Rado Riha develops in his reading of the Kantian critique.[18] Riha shows how reason has to criticize itself, to make the constitution of objectivity through the faculty of understanding first of all possible. In the process of this self-criticism, reason also enables itself to appear in the empirical realm: namely as the present absence of a truth-fiction, the present absence of an absolute, or, in Kantian terms, the present absence of ideas of reason. This appearance of an idea in the empirical realm Riha calls a de-realization of the world, a de-realization of reality. The eyes of the spectators of the French Revolution, Riha concludes, de-realize the world in this sense. Now this de-realization is part of the constitution of objectivity, part of the work of reason. The objectivity based on this de-realization is the same objectivity as before, with the minimal change that it now appears in the light of the idea, a minimal change that changes everything.

With Riha, and modifying his argument for our purposes, we could say that in the eyes of the enthusiastic spectators the shimmer of the idea is mirrored, but this very idea is nothing less than a de-realization of reality. The de-realization of reality is not only the work of the idea, it also enables us to see that there is more in this world than we are able to see. There is something present as absent, and this is, in the scene of art, the universality of space and time as equally addressing one, not as a physical presence, but rather as the present absence of this universality. So this universality for all does not exist the way an empirical fact does; it emerges from the de-realization occurring before our eyes as inexistent (taking up another formulation of Riha's that refers back to Badiou) in the world.

Coming back to the spectator in Rancière, we have to shift this argument a bit. We could understand the Rancièrian spectator as someone who becomes a possible mirror of the idea of equality. Becoming a possible mirror of the idea of equality makes the spectator on the one hand part of an emancipatory process that is, on the other hand, not the direct, determined result of the work of art. The spectator does not experience a power in him as an individual, but he experiences the power of an idea that integrates him into a collective subjectivity. The point I want to make is: the work of art can be considered a de-realization of the order of the sensible, and this present absence integrates the individual spectator into a collective process of dis-identification. The de-realization has a universal address, it is embodied in the specific work of art, but it addresses everyone. The world of things, the world of the object is not all, there is more to it than we can grasp with our senses. Or: what we grasp with our senses is not all, there is more in it than what we grasp with our senses.

The art object displays this absence of a totality negatively, it is in the world and out of this world. It unfolds its effects only in the sensible, because it is a sensible object and claims to be a totality. It claims to be another total reality of space and time, but in this way it shows that the sensible we know is not all. In this, its negative effect, the work of art integrates the spectators. It integrates them directly, because of their physical presence, which is directly connected to this split in the order of the sensible.

When Jacotot's book unfolds its emancipatory effect through the help of the will of the ignorant schoolmaster, the art object offers this universal address as a concrete being that realizes its de-realization in its concrete presence, and it therefore unfolds its emancipatory effect everywhere it is. So this scene is not the scene of the two, but the scene of the concrete presence of anyone.

The affirmation of this moment (or of the scene of art) would be the affirmation of a collectivizing moment of the idea of equality. This neither leads us to a political party, nor turns the artwork into some kind of master of emancipation. It still does not lead us to a political scene. But it is a mediator between the individual scene of emancipation and the political, collective subjectivation.

This, one could understand, is Rancière's claim: today we have to start from the split in the sensible and see that the normal order of the sensible is not all. The sensible is the realm of the objective, and art is its split, and this split in being is the only moment that allows us to become subjects, starting from an absence, a present absence in space and time. Which will then allow us to learn that objective reality is always constituted through a kernel of non-objective reality.

Art is, then, the most radical education in emancipation, because it is an objective education: the scene of art is concerned with a de-realizing object. We have historical confidence through communist moments, and we have individual confidence through intellectual emancipation. But what we also have to learn is that objectivity is incomplete, and that in this incompleteness we inexist as subjects. It is through this objectivity that we can learn that we, not being objects, can become subjects. And it is from this breaking up of objectivity, which we can realize in events like those in Tahrir Square, that we can learn that we inexist in that what is called the impossible. Because, as a real spectator, we always take part in what is happening without being part of it.[19]

1 See Peter Hallward, "In Egypt and Tunisia the will of the people is not a hollow cliché," *The Guardian*, January 31, 2011; accessed http://www.guardian.co.uk/commentisfree/2011/jan/31/egypt-tunisia-will-of-the-people

2 In Badiou, this is of paramount importance and is developed through different texts. In *The Communist Hypothesis* he condenses the relation between the political event and the impossible in the following way: "[...] with respect to a situation or a world, an event paves the way for the possibility of what from the limited perspective of the make-up of this situation or the legality of this world – is strictly impossible." Cf. Alain Badiou, *The Communist Hypothesis* (London / New York: Verso 2009), 243. An excellent account of the relation between politics and the impossible in Badiou's philosophy is given by Bruno Bosteels, "Logics of Change. From Potentiality to Inexistence," in *Beyond Potentialities? Politics between the Possible and the Impossible*, ed. Mark Potocnik, Frank Ruda, Jan Voelker (Zürich: diaphanes, 2011), 79-101. The dissociation of this concept of politics from theories like that of Foucault is shown with exactness by Frank Ruda: "Back to the Factory. A Plea for a Renewal of Concrete Analysis of Concrete Situations," *Beyond Potentialities?*, 39-54.

3 Cf. Alain Badiou, "Tunisie, Egypte : quand un vent d'est balaie l'arrogance de l'Occident," *Le Monde*, February 18, 2011; accessed http://www.lemonde.fr/idees/article/2011/02/18/tunisie-egypte-quand-un-vent-d-est-balaie-l-arrogance-de-l-occident_1481712_3232.html

4 Jacques Rancière: *The Emancipated Spectator*, trans. Gregory Elliott (London / New York: Verso, 2009).

5 Jacques Rancière: *The Ignorant Schoolmaster. Five Lessons in Intellectual Emancipation*, trans. Kristin Ross (Stanford, CA: Stanford University Press, 1991).

6 ibid., 41.

7 ibid., 18

8 Immanuel Kant, "An answer to the question: What is enlightenment?," in *Immanuel Kant: Practical Philosophy*, trans. and ed. by Mary J. Gregor (Cambridge: Cambridge University Press, 1996), 11-22; here 17. Again, I can only allude to the Badiousian use of the term "courage." But the differences in the peculiar conception of courage Badiou develops would demand another article.

9 Jacques Rancière, "Communists without Communism?," in *The Idea of Communism*, ed. Costas Douzinas and Slavoj Žižek (London / New York: Verso, 2010), 167-177; here 169.

10 For this, see also Jacques Rancière, "Communism: From Actuality to Inactuality," in *Jacques Rancière, Dissensus. On Politics and Aesthetics*, trans. Steven Corcoran (London / New York: Continuum, 2010), 76–83.

11 Jacques Rancière, "Communists without Communism?," 173.

12 Ibid., 176f.

13 Jacques Rancière, *The Emancipated Spectator*, 13.

14 Ibid., 73.

15 Ibid., 72.

16 Ibid., 16f.

17 Immanuel Kant, "The Contest of the Faculties," in *Kant: Political Writings*, 2d ed., ed. Hans Reiss (Cambridge: Cambridge University Press, 1991), 176-191; here 182.

18 I am primarily referring to an unpublished paper Rado Riha gave at a workshop 2010 in Berlin, at the Free University. Parts as well as extensions of the argument can also be found in Rado Riha, "Kant et la subjectivation de la réalité," in *Filozofski vestnik*, vol. XXVII, no. 2 (2006), 103–119.

19 I would like to thank Jason E. Smith for his very helpful, critical and friendly comments on this text.

5

PAPER VOICES

Claire Fontaine

Carpenters, child workers, seamstresses and artisans are not the usual inhabitants of philosophy books, but we often encounter them in Rancière's writings. This opaque mass of proletarians that threatens every attempt to write about universal emancipation usually remains on the edge of the page, discretely consuming the writer's desire to speak for everyone. They silently embody writers' worst danger: it's easy to turn into a pitiful Don Quixote, writing letters to people that do not know they are these letters' addressees, any more than Alondza Lorenzo knows that she is called Dulcinea and who, anyway, cannot even read.

In the section of *The Flesh of Words* entitled "The Literature of Philosophers," Rancière delivers a merciless diagnosis: the exemplary hero of every epistemological revolution is a professional fighter of windmills. And the knowledge of this fact led Althusser directly to the eternal night of madness, which his writings were supposed to help him conjure away. All of Althusser's *oeuvre*—Rancière says—is entirely marked by the typical dread of the Marxist intellectual who has fallen prey to politics: the fear of making literature, sending letters with no recipients, or being the voice that cries in the desert. Speaking to the void, haranguing an imaginary crowd that never massed together or becoming oneself a crowd and performing all the different characters oneself are frightening risks that must be exorcized through the rigor of theory. Although Lenin is described by Althusser as the little man standing alone on the plain of history, his solitude takes place within history, where one is somehow protected by a tight fabric of questions and answers that will always seem to keep us warm. But will they really? Who are these answers and questions truly written for? For the proletarians that we cannot be but that we can write about, even if we then run the risk of drowning their voices when doing so? Because, as Althusser says in *For Marx*, writing is a way of paying a debt, precisely the debt of not being born a proletarian and not being born illiterate. But the silence of infamous men can be deafening, it can fill any speculation with an insane urge for action and turn any reasonable theoretical activity into the fury of organization. And if there are no actual people around to organize, then the fury will turn toward the letters on the page.

The abbreviations AIE, PP1, PP2, element one, element two, that infest Althusser's letters to John Lewis, Rancière notices, are talking concepts: it is they who speak instead of the subjects. This Althusserian typography—he continues—is a dramaturgy, a form of theatre, and whilst populating these pages it embodies the classes and the class struggle, Marxism-Leninism, the workers' movement and other characters. Althusser's typography is also a topology in the dramatic sense: it is an *incarnation* that brings the interlocutor of the book's page to existence, a device for transubstantiating letters and signs. And yet something resists the docile coming and going between concepts and writing, something wrecks the mechanism: the Lumpenproletariat cannot find a place in this theory for its placeless existence, and Rancière condemns Althusser's position on the problem. He writes: "despite the praiseworthy efforts made to give it an economic-social materialistic genealogy, the Lumpenproletariat is first of all a phantasmagoria, a stage name, the theatrical embodiment of all the distances of scholarly speech, the generic name of nonmeaning, of disconnection, of non-relation."[1]

If it is impossible to annihilate any distance between reality and thought, Althusser's parable proves that it is instead possible to fight a total war against nonsense and to lose one's mind while doing so.

*

Coming back to Rancière's method, and the objects of his interest, we can see that if he stigmatizes Althusser's organizing obsession and terror for those aspects of life that are without reason, mad, and that can't be absorbed by a political grid, it is because Rancière is attracted by the poetic consequences of this disorder and by its political causes.

The concept of the "distribution of the sensible" that gives the title to his best-known book from 2000 is already at work in several of his previous writings. We can read in a note at the end of the 1997 "Preface" to *The Nights of Labor* that in 1981, when the book was first published, its aim was to oppose both the historian's positivism and the so-called "nouveaux philosophes" who in the late 1970s set about detailing the dangers and crimes provoked by those thinkers who had envisaged the possibility of changing the world. Describing the wanderings and the need for poetry felt by a handful of proletarians that were twenty years old around 1830 and spent many of their nights talking and writing is a first way to establish a different distribution of the sensible. The "proletarian night" explores the grey area where the workers can become clandestine intellectuals, nocturnal writers, and thereby no longer coincide with their stereotype. Confronted with these hybrid figures, official intellectuals and orthodox representatives of the working class feel equally uncomfortable. It was worth rescuing these archives from their oblivion just to awaken this discomfort again.

Rancière is not only interested in the tactics at work in the construction of historical tales, in the borders violently traced and re-traced through different revolutions between history and literature, science and arts; he is interested in how the crowd invades the page, and in how the written word influences the body of the ignorant reader. That's why he underlines the systematic expulsion of the chaos that poor people's words bring inside the architecture of a book. Giving the status of meaningful words to expressions that are normally considered parasitical noise and meaningless sound is the recurrent philosophical gesture in Rancière's oeuvre.

In *The Names of History*, for example, he observes with skepticism that the Mediterranean Sea's becoming the subject of Braudel's book rather than a king or a hero is above all a poetic operation—and not an innocent one. In his preface to *The Mediterranean and the Mediterranean World in the Age of Philip II*, Braudel develops the reasons for the *longue durée* approach that characterized the Annales School. One should mistrust—he says—the history told while it's still burning, told from the perspective of how it has been felt and lived by its contemporaries, whose lives are as short as ours, because it is shot through with their anger, their dreams and their illusions. (There seems to be a need for cooling down the passionate aspect of the historical event and for zooming out from the limited scale of the individual life.) In the sixteenth century—Braudel affirms—the poor people's Renaissance takes place, and at that point the poor, the humble, start to write relentlessly about others and themselves. But he continues:

> All these precious records give a somewhat distorted view,
> invading that lost time and taking up an excessive amount
> of space in it. A historian, reading some papers of Philip II
> as if he were in his place and time, would find himself
> transported into a bizarre world, missing a dimension. A
> world of vivid passions, certainly, but a blind world, as any

living world must be, as ours is, oblivious of the deep currents of history, of those living waters on which our frail
barks are tossed like Rimbaud's drunken boat.[2]

This is an account of an expulsion, of the re-establishment of the
long-lasting order of the dispassionate historian. How much did
these poor people write of their anger and their passion? How many
of their letters actually invaded the king's desk? And why did the
historian need so badly to clear them out of his own version of history? What kind of depth is the one that poor people's words don't
reach and what is the surface where they proliferate? All we get to
know, Rancière says, is the absence of all this clutter. Poor people
are treated like nothing more than the impertinent messengers of
a disorder that the theoretician needs to contain: the poor of the
Platonic myth—like the Lumpenproletariat in Althusser's theory—
aren't defined by social categories but are names for a relationship to
non-truth. They speak blindly, too close to the event, since the very
fact of speaking is an event for them. And if they write "relentlessly,"
they do so because *they are not supposed to write*, and they insist
on causing this confusion that troubles the historian whose "good"
object is the silence of the compact masses.

We listen to contraband intellectuals and dreaming workers
with more pleasure when they keep their mouth shut, comments
Rancière in *The Nights of Labor*.[3] Some words and some speeches
are unwelcome everywhere, and it is precisely these that Rancière
patiently collects from archives. The waste, the debris that can't
be metabolized by other people's theory are the main object of his
own, with the fragility and the problems that come with them.

Methodologically speaking, Rancière is not immune from the
temptation of systematizing his objects, and it becomes then unclear
what use the reader should make of these rescued voices that tell us
what no one wanted to hear. Moreover, a work of patient demolition
of the philosophical posture runs between the lines of several of his
major books. The criticism of intellectual authority is always justified
by the distribution of the sensible that made it possible. Plato, Althusser,
Braudel, Bourdieu, Sartre, Marx and many others are proved complicit
with a desire to obliterate the voices of proletarians or assimilate them
within a philosophical system whose final aim is to absolve its creator
and not put him in touch with his real contradictions.

But what are these real contradictions, actually? Contrary to
what it might look like at first glance, Rancière's prose doesn't aim
to render moral justice but to redistribute complexity and precision.

An example of his curiously materialistic approach is provided by the place of words in his philosophy: "the ailment of politics," he writes in *The Names of History*, "is first the ailment of words. There are too many words that designate nothing other than the very targets against which they place weapons in the killers' hand."[4]

Because the legitimacy of a power is a matter of the distribution of the sensible, what changes a leader into a tyrant is a shift in the general sensibility, a simultaneous agreement on what is intolerable, the possibility of naming things and facts differently. These transformations take place in the space of words, which is undivided from the space of politics. Words have effects on bodies and objects. This is the fulcrum of the introductory chapter of *The Flesh of Words* where, for once, Rancière takes Plato's side: the Phaedrus' critique of the vain portrait of the logos presented by written, mute, letters is justified:

> The problem is not that the resemblance [of the text to the speech] is unfaithful, but that it is too faithful, still attached to what has been said when already it should be elsewhere, near where the meaning of what has been said must speak. The written letter is like a silent painting that retains on its body the movement that animates the logos and bring it to its destination.[5]

The destinations are, of course, the active body of the speaker and the receptive body of the listener, but the journey between the word and the flesh is uncertain and contradictory. Therefore the letter as a form is approached as the physical trace of the invisible miracle moving the text from the page into the mouth and mind of the reader. In this sense the ignorant schoolmaster's adventure is essential within the economy of Rancière's *oeuvre*, because Jacotot represents the anti-Althusser: the inventor of the universal teaching method is the total opposite of the pedantic pedagogue who disguises the ordinary exercise of knowledge as the extraordinary performance of the erudite. Jacotot tells the story of people becoming literate outside of and against the vertical teacher-student relationship. Reading, recognizing the letters and the meaning of words, according to Jacotot, is an activity that the illiterate already know how to perform, but in a different field. There is, in his system, a competence of the "ignorant" that can always be used as a starting point for learning anything else. Since the day we were born, we have been translators, as Jacotot himself spells out in *La langue maternelle*:

> The child is surrounded by objects that speak to him, all
> at once, in different languages; he must study them sep-
> arately and together; they have no relationship and often
> contradict each other. He can make nothing of all the
> idioms in which nature speaks to him—through his eyes,
> his touch, through all his senses—simultaneously. He must
> repeat often to remember so many absolutely arbitrary
> signs… What great attention is necessary for all that![6]

If the motif of the world as a hieroglyph to interpret is not new, the declination Jacotot uses and Rancière analyses in turn are intriguing: we all learn our mother tongue without teachers, and we all become capable of navigating the world through the lesson of things and creatures surrounding us. The cohabitation with confusion and changes within the distribution of the sensible appear as vital necessities: all knowledge has a common measure and is part of the non-hierarchical experience of life that everyone shares. Once the border between culture and the rest of the human competences is erased, knowledge and expression become immediately accessible. Jacotot thought all disciplines on the same level: the arbitrariness of language and the resistance of material in the hands can both teach an important lesson and can be equally efficient supports for the transmission of an intensity. We read in *The Ignorant Schoolmaster* that:

> The artist's emancipatory lesson, opposed on every
> count to the professor's stultifying lesson, is this: each
> one of us is an artist to the extent that he carries out
> a double process; he is not content to be a mere jour-
> neyman but wants to make all work a means of expres-
> sion, and he is not content to feel something but tries
> to impart it to others. The artist needs equality as the
> explicator needs inequality. And therefore he designs the
> model of a reasonable society where the very thing that
> is outside reason—matter, linguistic signs—is traversed
> by reasonable will: that of telling the story and making
> others feel the ways in which we are similar to them.[7]

It's in the nineteenth century that these ideas began to circulate, when the disorder of politics disorganized the hierarchy of knowledge and vice versa. It was the shift towards what Rancière calls in *The Mute Word* "the expressive regime":

Every configuration of sensible properties can be
assimilated to a disposition of signs, therefore to a
manifestation of language in its poetic original state. And
this double level applies to everything… This power of
language immanent to every object can be interpreted
in a mystical way, like the young philosophers or the
German poets did, who were always repeating Kant's
sentence on the nature being a poem written in an
encrypted language, and like Novalis assimilated the
study of materials to the old science of signatures. But we
can also rationalize it and make it into the witness of the
fact that mute things carry the trace of human activity.[8]

The poet becomes "the one who formulates the poetical aspect of things." It's tempting to compare this turn with the change in the distribution of the sensible caused by the appearance of the ready-made in the 20th century in the domain of the visual arts, when the artist became the indicator of the "personal coefficient of art" contained in each object, that is, the arithmetic relation between "what is unexpressed but was projected" and "what was unintentionally expressed." (Duchamp presented this conception of the creative process at the meeting of the American Federation of the Arts in Houston in April 1957, in an incredible panel that included Rudolph Arnheim, Gregory Bateson and Duchamp himself, who introduced himself as "a poor artist.")

*

If the lesson of the poor artist points toward the society of the equality of intelligences, it's because his very element is disorder, because his space of work is contiguous to the whateverness of everyday life, sometimes even indistinguishable from it. In *Aesthetics and its Discontents*, Rancière describes aesthetics as we know it, and as it emerged two centuries ago, as the "thought of the new disorder."[9] There is a link, a homonymy, between the distinction of concepts and social distinction, for "clearly in the confusion or the distinction of aesthetics what is at stake is the social order and its transformations."[10] This was blatantly true in many social movements but exemplarily demonstrated by the Italian insurrection of 1977. Umberto Eco, who was at that time writing columns in several newspapers, remarked in one of them that the language of the divided self and the proliferation of messages organized on the basis of new codes was understood and perfectly reproduced by groups that were totally unfamiliar with high culture, that hadn't read Céline or Apollinaire, and had reached that language through music, posters, parties and concerts, while the high culture that used to understand the language of the divided self when spoken in the aseptic theoretical laboratory didn't understand it when it was spoken by the masses. Eco:

> In other words the cultivated man used to make fun
> of the bourgeois who in the museum, in front of a
> woman with three eyes and graffiti without a defined
> shape, would say "I don't understand what it rep-
> resents." Now the same cultivated man is facing a
> generation that expresses itself by elaborating women
> with three eyes and graffiti without a defined shape,
> and he says "I don't understand what it means." What
> seemed acceptable as an abstract utopia, a hypothesis
> in a laboratory, seems unacceptable when it presents
> itself in flesh and bones.[11]

This disorienting incarnation, the indomitable heterogeneity of the real uprising, the remainder that remains on this side of theory, even after the acknowledgment of the change of the distribution of the sensible, are both the center of Rancière's theory and the abyss into which it sinks. In *Short Voyages to the Land of the People*, the problem is exposed in all its clarity. There is no point in waiting for the revolution to come from visits by the intellectual class to the proletarian regions: these tourists only bring the message of separation. It's a story of mourning what the utopian poems and writings export, a mourning of the impossible social link between rich and poor which is made, Rancière insists, of the only thing that can make a social link: love.[12] Cultivated and well-intentioned intellectuals try to share with the poor the very word that is the cause and image of their separation from them. The story of Rainer Maria Rilke and Martha, the poor bohemian girl, is an example of this tragedy. Their love is impossible in the precarious theatre of the reality they can share, made of sleepless nights spent walking hand-in-hand in the desolation of the faubourgs. But Martha can become, once abandoned, a literary character, a mute source of inspiration, so that the poem is the very place where transfiguration is reached through the desertion of her body.

At this point we have the right to feel puzzled. We begin to understand that the voices of the poor that we have encountered through Rancière's books are still made of paper and that the correspondence between writing and reality, between the visual and the textual is a dangerous domain of shadows. In the transcription of a conference on Mallarmé and Broodthaers given in January, 2004, Rancière dives into a deeply materialistic analysis of Broodthaers' practice that he interprets as a refusal of the equivalence between words and forms. Rancière takes as an example Broodthaers' re-writing of La Fontaine's poem "The Crow and the Fox." The words and verses of the poem are sent back by the artist to a school-like universe: "The D is bigger than the T. All the Ds must have the same length. The downstroke and the oval must have the same slope as that of the A." And this is all the written story will positively tell us about concrete reality: the story of the shape of the written letters. Letters that Jacotot's locksmith student already compared to the familiar forms of his profession: the letter O was "the round" and the letter L "the corner plate." What follows is the record of the loss we are exposed to when dealing with the text, even ourselves in this very moment:

> The Crow and the Fox are absent. I can hardly remember
> them. I have forgotten the paws and the hands, the
> games and the costumes, the voices and the colors, the
> treacherousness and the vanity. The painter was all colors
> and the architect was made out of stone. The crow and
> the fox were made out of printed characters.

The absence of the objects and the creatures leaves room only for the mute shape of the letters and the black of the ink. Broodthaers is also probably talking about the commodity, about reification, the experience of feeling in good company when surrounded by objects and being faced with the problematic coexistence of images and words on the surface of advertising. Broodthaers himself posed in 1971 as a model for Van Laack Shirts, whose firm was owned by a German couple of collectors, Rolf and Erika Hoffmann. The advertisement was printed in the German magazine *Der Spiegel*, and on his own copy Broodthaers wrote: "What shall one think of the links between art, advertisement and business? MB (the director)."

Without wanting to give an answer to this question whose pertinence doesn't even need to be discussed, we will try to conclude with a hypothesis. If Rancière's theory remains exposed to the danger of its own paradoxes, it might all the same achieve some coherence on another level. But it does so only when it doesn't explicitly revolve around contemporary art. It finds a tone and a language that can coexist with the desire for freedom without showing the way to follow and without prescribing any ethical position—leaving us, indeed, alone in the deceptive company of words.

[1] Jacques Rancière, *The Flesh of Words: The Politics of Writing*. trans. Charlotte Mandell, (Stanford: Stanford University Press, 2004), 139.

[2] Fernand Braudel, *On History*, trans. Sarah Matthews (Chicago: University of Chicago Press, 1980), 4.

[3] Jacques Rancière, *The Nights of Labor*, trans. John Drury (Philadelphia: Temple UP, 1989), 14.

[4] Jacques Rancière, *The Names of History: On the Poetics of Knowledge*, trans. Hassan Melehy (Minneapolis: The University of Minnesota Press, 1994),19.

[5] Rancière, *The Flesh of Words*, 3.

[6] Jacques Rancière, *The Ignorant Schoolmaster*, trans. Kristin Ross (Stanford: Stanford University Press, 1991), 51.

[7] Ibid., 70-71.

[8] Jacques Rancière, *La parole muette: essai sur les contradictions de la littérature* (Paris: Hachette, 1998), 41.

[9] Jacques Rancière, *Aesthetics and its Discontents*, trans. Steven Corcoran (Malden: Polity, 2009), 13.

[10] Ibid., 4.

[11] U. Eco, "Il laboratorio in piazza," *L'Espresso*, April 10, 1977; our translation.

[12] "The language needed to bind the classes together is the language of the bond in general. What is missing between the poor and the educated is what makes for a bond in general, among the rich as among the poor: love." See Jacques Rancière, *Short Voyages to the Land of the People*, trans. James B. Swenson (Stanford: Stanford UP, 2003), 78.

6

THE MASTER IN HIS PLACE: JACQUES RANCIÈRE AND THE POLITICS OF THE WILL

Jason E. Smith

There is nothing the schoolmaster can hide from him, and nothing he can hide from the master's gaze. The circle forbids cheating, and above all that great cheat: *I can't, I don't understand.* There is nothing to understand. Everything is in the book.

Jacques Rancière, *The Ignorant Schoolmaster*

1. There is a certain assumption made by even the most perspicuous readers of Rancière that, in the words of one of those readers, his work in all of its phases and fields of intervention (history, philosophy, literary and film theory, aesthetics) is motivated by a "subversion of mastery."[1] I want to begin this essay by arguing that, for Rancière, it is in fact the presence of the master in the pedagogical scene that makes possible the unfolding of the emancipatory process. He or she is guided by the maxim that must orient any egalitarian sequence: you can, the master asserts, precisely because "there is nothing to understand." Far from being banished from the process of emancipation, the master plays a decisive role whose exact effects we must examine.

Let's begin with Rancière's explicit formulations concerning the place of the master in the community of equals. What we witness in these formulations is not a deposing of the master in the name of a libertarian pedagogy or a proposal for a popular "self"-education to be undertaken on the basis of the abolition of the pedagogical scene and its structural poles of teacher and student. Rancière does not mince words here. What he outlines is not the suppression of the master or the emergence of an "equality" between teacher and student that echoes the flexible organization of the contemporary production process and behind whose affirmations of egalitarianism lurk what was once called the "tyranny of structurelessness."[2] What Rancière proposes instead is a rearticulation of the place of the master in the scene of pedagogy. We find there a master who is not identified as the possessor of knowledge or as the measure of intelligence, but as a presence that "absolutely commands" the will of the student, who must in turn necessarily "obey" that of the master.[3] The emancipatory scene is not founded on the deposing of the master, but on the splitting off of the place of mastery from the possession of knowledge. If an egalitarian pedagogy begins from the assumption that all intelligences are equal—that there is no distinction between the rational, methodical thought of the master and the groping experimentation of the student who compares facts and recounts stories—this equality can only be *enforced*, that is, be real, through the paradoxical submission of the student's will to that of the teacher's: "In the experimental situation Jacotot created, the student was linked to a will, Jacotot's, and to an intelligence, the book's—the two entirely distinct. We will call the known and maintained difference of the two relations—the act of an intelligence obeying only itself even while the will obeys another will—*emancipation*."[4]

The schoolmaster is ignorant but he still exercises a will over the student, and this command is, as Rancière reiterates, "unconditional." Because pedagogy cannot be institutionalized, the master who commands the scene of instruction is identified with the place or name of the Father. The ignorant schoolmaster's "place" is

> where the unconditional exigency of the will is incar-
> nated. Unconditional exigency: the emancipatory father
> is not a simple, good-natured pedagogue; he is an intrac-
> table master. The emancipatory commandment knows
> no compromises. It absolutely commands of a subject
> what it supposes it is capable of commanding itself.[5]

There is an analogy, perhaps lazy or misleading, linking Rancière's distinction between the person of the master and the "place" of mastery with Claude Lefort's too-well known definition of the democratic form of politics as founded on the emptying out of the place of power, and the establishment of a contingent link between the place of power itself and whatever or whoever occupies that place. Rancière emphasizes this obliquely at certain moments in his account of Jacotot's theory, when he stresses that in certain circumstances the position of the master could be occupied by another student ("each ignorant person could become for another ignorant person the master"[6]) in a kind of community of mutual masters (or slaves[7]) or perhaps by the "constraint of the situation" whose "urgency demands destroying the states of explicative progression."[8] You can even occupy the place of the master yourself, in a certain type of self-mastery, if you are "propelled by [your] own desire."[9] If "a person may need a master when his own will is not strong enough," as Rancière qualifies it ("may"), what is absolutely necessary in the scene of emancipation is the presence of a force, a compulsion and an urgency applied to the will of the student in order that the student assume responsibility for his or her own intelligence, a will that compels the student to obey, paradoxically, his or her own intelligence alone.

What the master—whether teacher, fellow student, or the pressure of events—requires of the student is simply "attention." The task of the master is to compel attention, which is to say to *verify* that the path taken by the student—a path that is not the *hodos* of a methodical procedure, but the rigorous straying of an intelligence attentive to facts and their combination—is chosen and followed with discipline. This discipline is defined first and foremost as a staying close to itself of the act of thought, a "reflection" in which the intelligence—before the production of any positive knowledge—is conscious of its own activity and "knows its own power."[10] This task of verification, in which the master merely observes and compels attention, is supplemented by a more hands-on application of the will: the master must "demand speech"[11] from an intelligence that will otherwise remain unaware of its own power or will have "given up [*se délaissait*],"[12] announcing "I cannot" before sinking into silence.

The name for the will's renunciation of itself is *contempt*. Society, Rancière argues, is founded on just such a contempt for oneself and for others. To be social is to succumb to distraction. But distraction is not, as the term implies, a mere loss of tension or vigilance, a spacing out or dispersal of the will. To renounce one's own power is an *act*: it is a "perversion" of the will. Just as for Kant so-called "radical" evil could not be attributed to the triumph of the pathological or sensible over reason and the will but was understood, to the contrary, as a manifestation of a positive wickedness that actively wills the worst, so here distraction is not a mere "torpor of the flesh," but a veritable "*act* of the mind underestimating its own power."[13] In this sense, we can understand society and its distribution of capacities and qualifications to be founded on both contempt for oneself and one another and on a *passion* for inequality: not a succumbing to the dead weight of social division, but a furious will to implement it. It is a passion shot through with fear, fear first of all of oneself and one's power, "fear in the face of what a reasonable being owes to itself."[14] It is an anxiety before the infinite, before the "infinite task" the practice of equality requires and unleashes in the world. This task is infinite because the infinite exists only in act, that is, in the act of its verification. It cannot be achieved through the production or founding of an institution, but only through the resumption of its act of rupture with every institution. The infinite task of emancipation must be clearly distinguished, however, from its double or "ape" (the final chapter of *The Ignorant Schoolmaster* goes by the title "The Emancipator and his Monkey [*Singe*]"), the infinite task implied by the idea of progress. For there are, in fact, two orders of the infinite: the infinity of emancipation, in its endless dialectic of presupposition and verification of equality, and the incremental acquisitions and accumulation of progress, whose every step restores the very distance it claims to bridge, and whose "reasoned progress" is tantamount to "an indefinitely reproduced mutilation."[15] The claim to institute emancipation, which is say, to have done with it, can only ever give rise to a "ploy, a school or a military unit."[16]

2. What this conception of emancipation proposes is not a solution to the riddles of revolutionary politics, but a particularly dramatic separation between the logic of society and the immanent rationality of egalitarian practices. The very idea of society, in Rancière's account of Jacotot's theory, is founded on the "primal passion" of contempt as I have already laid it out: contempt for others, contempt for oneself. This contempt takes the specific form of a denial or foreclosure of the axiom whose positing triggers and orients the aleatory course of emancipation: the assertion, indemonstrable but eminently verifiable, that there is only one intelligence. This contempt is not something to which one merely falls prey. The denial of the equality of intelligence requires an effort of the will. Prostration before power is not only the effect of the forces of social gravity, the tug that pulls a body into its assigned place, role and task. Society is founded on an originary division of intelligences, a division between what gets called reason and the merely sensible knowledge produced by the comparison and translation between facts. This production of reason through a division of intelligence is irrational, because arbitrary. Rancière even speaks of the "fiction" of the social. If the order of society has a certain logic—what in *Disagreement* will be called the "logic" of the police—the foundation and reproduction of this order is, in turn, absolutely contingent, arbitrary,

and unjustifiable. The reproduction of this order requires coercion. Society is "war." But: "by the term 'war,' let us not think here of any fatal clash of material forces."[17] The war that Rancière speaks of here, before and perhaps instead of being a confrontation between materially determined social forces—class struggle, to make things absolutely clear—is a mode of speech, a form of mastery that speaks not in order to "demand speech" (as the emancipatory "father" does), but in order to silence, that is, to explain [*expliquer*] why it is that you cannot speak: "It makes its goal the other's silence, the absence of reply, the plummeting of minds into the material aggregation of consent."[18]

There can be no struggle undertaken in the name of another, more egalitarian society. For, as we have seen, the name society is, for Rancière's Jacotot, by definition an order of inequality, founded on a division not of labor, first and foremost, but of intelligences. If the Marxist inflection of the worker's movement has always conceived of the real movement of emancipation as the production, through struggle, of another society—a society that would, once rationally constructed, spell the end of the political and give birth to the administration of things—the communism proposed by Jacotot is the formation of a community of emancipated individuals, not the abolition, by a determined class, of the society of classes:

> There cannot be a class of the emancipated, an assembly
> or a society of the emancipated. But any individual can
> always, at any moment, be emancipated and emancipate
> someone else, announce to others the practice and add
> to the number of people who know themselves as such
> and who no longer play the comedy of inferior superiors.
> A society, a people, a state, will always be irrational.
> But one can multiply within these bodies the number of
> people who, as individuals, will make use of reason, and
> who, as citizens, will know how to seek the art of raving
> as reasonably as possible.[19]

Equality is refractory to the law. The practice of equality will never become the foundation of a new society. The power unleashed by the process of emancipation cannot, therefore, be understood as the constitutive power of a people, the force of whose actions alone posit and legitimate or guarantee the relative justness of a given social order. Insofar as the social order is arbitrary, and insofar as this arbitrariness is redoubled by the *déraison*—the raving of false reason—that attempts to rationalize the radical contingency of this order, society can be pronounced a fiction, which is also to say, a "machine." This active reason of equality, the intelligence that manifests itself through the attention of the will and is verified in the "material ideality"[20] of the book, cannot found another order, but must "circulate" within this machine, neither making it run nor shutting it down: "whoever forsakes the workings of the social machine has the opportunity to make the electrical energy of emancipation circulate."[21]

To circulate within the social machine is to leave its gears without grit. The process of emancipation occurs through a movement of separation, the taking of a distance. Rancière insists that the practice of emancipation, because its own rationality necessarily breaks with, while remaining indifferent to, the social order, falls nowhere on the classical scale or continuum that measures the intensity of social transformation. Emancipation will never appear "on the program of reformist parties, nor should intellectual emancipation be inscribed on the banners of sedition."[22] Rancière even underlines that individuals—by which we should understand, the minimal cell of master-pupil-book—can pursue the infinite task of emancipation within society while "respecting" that society itself. But that respect, it should be made clear, signals less an identification with that order than a wary distance assumed from within; respect necessarily implies, in these terms, a refusal to "believe" in the social fiction.[23] Through this gap between respect and belief, the current of emancipation runs.

Jacotot's and Rancière's separation of the rational infinitization of emancipation and the irrationality of "reasoned progress" represents an impasse that Rancière's work subsequent to *The Ignorant Schoolmaster* will attempt to breach. For if the logic of the social order is here identified with a perversion of the will Rancière already calls consensus,[24] there seems to be no corresponding moment of *dissensus* in this account, in which the configuration of the sensible— the contingency of a given "partition"—is suspended and, perhaps, displaced. *Disagreement* is entirely devoted to notching the site where the process of emancipation, politics [*la politique*], intersects with and interrupts the machine of the police order [*la police*]: the political [*le politique*], or in other iterations, the community or communism, is the name for these scenes or "moments." But even with this novel account in the later work of the retroactive inscription of the "social effects" of politics, the propositions regarding the nature of the emancipatory process in Rancière's account have given rise to a series of objections, all of which we might file, to echo Rancière's break after 1968 with the milieu of Althusserianism and the politics of the PCF as well as his subsequent polemics with the ex-Maoist "new philosophers" in the mid-to-late 1970s, under the charge of *leftism*. Let me quickly resume these objections: the political overdetermination of knowledge in his critique of scientism, the symbolic conception of social war as the production of an exclusion or silence rather than a confrontation between material forces or classes, a transhistorical concept of the social that is both dehistoricized and can account neither for transformations of power nor for the isolating of weak links, a refusal to locate any communist tendencies immanent to a given form of power and a corresponding bracketing of questions of strategy—which might locate where force is most effectively deployed in a given conjuncture—and class composition—which might locate which actors prefigure forms of struggle and organization that can produce a transition to a new society. In short, leftism in this particular configuration would amount to a *voluntarism*—a folding back of revolutionary initiative entirely on the will of the individual to be emancipated, without regard for the material conditions that determine the capacities of a given will. What is more, and perhaps worse: all subjection, in turn, is an affair of the will and perversion. All servitude is voluntary.

3. In a remarkable essay published more or less contemporaneously with his book on Jacotot, Rancière recounts the experiences and ambitions of the young workers who, fresh from the insurrectionary experiences of 1830—and in particular from the implementation of the modern strike as a tactic and figure of struggle that transforms material conflict into a "rational demonstration" —attempt to bridge the separation between the process of emancipation on the one hand and the social distribution of capacities on the other. Where Jacotot had insisted on the *dissociation* necessary to trigger a properly egalitarian sequence and the rising up of a common or community, this community must remain "inconsistent," as Rancière puts it, voided of any substantial foundation, and contracted into the repeated *acts* of its instantiation. The act involved here is characterized by its discreteness: what is put into play in this punctual act, however long it lasts, is the articulation of two wills, that of the teacher who refuses to explain and a student who refuses to assume his or her "master" has anything to explain and so turns to the "thing in common"[25] standing between them, in which alone the singleness of the intellect can be verified.

Community is therefore founded on the assumption or axiom that intelligence is one, and the corresponding "proof" of this singleness of the intellect, its being shared universally and equally, in the materiality, the thingliness of the book, or more precisely, the "material ideality" of language itself. If intelligence is one, it is not collective: it is appropriated each time in a singular configuration between wills and the thing that measures the distance between them. Equality can be made actual, "realized," but this effectivity can, as I have already underlined, never take the form of a social or public institution. This is why it "takes place, but has no place"[26]; why it occurs, but is always missing from its place. Here, then, it is necessary to distinguish between the act and the actual. The *real* of emancipation can never take the form of what is actual, that is, the filling out of a sketched possible. The emancipatory act is defined by its capacity to break with the Aristotelian schema of actualization: not a potentiality to be made manifest, but a double movement of presupposition and verification. The act is suspended between its status as axiom and as fact. Its punctuality is, rather, its recursivity; its presence, the tension between an always-prior assumption and indefinite process of verification.

Now it is precisely this separation between emancipatory act and social effects that is questioned by those workers who passed through the crucible of the revolt of 1830, who undertake to realize —or at least to hypothesize and experiment with—the "social inscription" of the egalitarian prescription, despite or in defiance of Jacotot's cautions. In his description of Jacotot's own itinerary of emancipation, Rancière underlines that it is Jacotot's experience of the French Revolution—and not just any moment of that sequence, but 1792–1793—that stands in the place of the "master," with the force of events ("the peril of the country") "engender[ing] … unknown capacities," whose "urgency demand[s] destroying the stages of explicative progression."[27] This aspect of Rancière's account of the relation between master and student has generally been overlooked; it puts a revolutionary sequence itself, a situation of "danger"—the arrayed counter-revolutionary forces besieging the revolutionary process—in the place of the master who conducts, leads and even enforces the emancipatory process in times of relative peace. The irruption of social war in 1830 may in fact play the same role here, of that pressure that, in the absence of a particular relation between will and will, demands of the workers as a collective force a type of speech, or to return to my own opening paragraphs, to the production of two statements: we can, because there is nothing to understand.

In *The Ignorant Schoolmaster*, Rancière stressed the importance of the fable of Menenius Agrippa in the discourse of the workers' emancipation movement, citing in particular the version and reading proposed by Pierre-Simon Ballanche in order to underline the performative contradiction between the content of the fable itself—Agrippa comes to the plebeians to explain to them the "reasons" for social inequality—and the scene or staging of the fable itself: in order for the plebeians to understand their subordination, they must be capable of understanding to begin with, that is, to share the space of speech and reason with those who deny them this very capacity. The workers fresh from the insurrectionary experience of 1830 read the fable differently. Or, they placed the emphasis not so much on the content of the speech and its presuppositions as on the "event" the precedes it:

> [They] shift the emphasis still again, the strong moment
> of the scene: no longer only from the content of the fable
> to the speaking situation which gave rise to it, but to that
> of the event that precedes this situation and imposes it. In
> order for Menenius Agrippa to compose his fable, it was
> necessary that the Plebeians withdraw to the Aventine,
> but also that they speak, give themselves a name, and
> make it understood [*fassent entendre*] that they are
> themselves speaking beings to whom one should speak
> [*il convient de venir parler*].[28]

The plebeians do not simply secede from the city, they also begin to speak, speak by giving themselves a name, a name by which they can be called to appear before an other, and be addressed. The emphasis here, it seems to me, is on the question of a certain deployment of force. The secession of the plebeians is not simply the suspension of the material relations that constitute the social strata of Roman society; it is also just as importantly the constitution of a "polemical site" (or "polemical space") where the root resonating in the adjective polemical—*polemos*—must be understood at once as an act of war and as space of litigiousness, a dispute between speaking beings that cannot be mediated by a given form of legality or settled by a third-party, by an arbitrator. The *polemos* produces a space common to the plebeians and the patricians in the very act of separation, and this space is to a certain extent *forced* on the patricians: they have no choice but to listen to *these people*, these people who only a moment before were capable only of signaling, through cries and moans, the abjection of the most common pleasure and the suffering of martyrless pain.

This is why Rancière suggests that the solution to the impasse posited by Jacotot requires reaching back for a moment prior to the fable, to what he calls in measured terms that nevertheless underline the conflictual dimension of the polemical moment of secession an "inaugural violence":

> The community of speaking beings founds its effectivity
> on a preliminary violence. The essence of this violence—
> foreign to every counting of the dead and wounded—
> is to render visible the invisible, to give a name to the
> anonymous, to make speech heard there where before
> only sound was perceived.[29]

To speak of violence here is to speak of what could be called a "transcendental violence," if by this we mean a violence that warps, deforms or reconfigures the conditions of phenomenality, "before" the occurrence of any empirical violence—including the violence of class warfare, whether in the form of the extortion of surplus-value in the hidden spaces of the factory or the very public forms of confrontation between classes in a material confrontation—in which the given actors and forms of activity are already identified, given. But we can also understand violence here to mean the manner in which the dominant forces in a given society are compelled to acknowledge the emergence of a new force in the space of social conflict, even if this acknowledgement takes the manifest form of a *Verneinung*. In the scene on the Aventine, the plebeians exercise a will; they impose their *collective* will on the dominant classes of Rome. Or, in Rancière's terms, what happens in the passage from the emancipatory scene in Jacotot's pedagogy to the exemplary scene of social "emancipation" is the transformation of a relation between two wills—"a will-to-say" on the part of the student, and a "will-to-hear" the speech of the student on the part of the master,[30] that is, to verify the student's "attention" by referring it to the materiality of the book—to the "staging of an obligation to hear [*entendre*]," where obligation refers not to a moral or juridical prescription, but to the undeniability of the presence of the plebeians (or the proletarians of the workers movement in their most insurrectionary moments), of their having the initiative, of their having instituted a polemical front at the heart of society.

Such "moments" are exceptional. The space they produce cannot hold out; and yet they inscribe "social effects." The form of effectivity manifested by the Aventine secession and all of the stagings of polemical moments since—it is a single history, unbroken yet discontinuous—cannot be the founding of an institution, but only the reconfiguration of the space of appearing. Such an account requires that the very concept of society be defined not as a system of needs, as the organization of production and the distribution of wealth that would be opposed to the "rationality" of the state, nor as the site of material forms of conflict, whether in the factory or in the streets; society is simply the name for the triage of social capacities, the splitting of the intelligence in two, the way the border between what appears and what stays muffled is policed by forces that range from agencies of the state to the "well-meaning" discourses of the Left and its proposed solutions to the social question.

The lingering question posed by Rancière's account of the social effectivity of the egalitarian prescription, however, is the role of the *master*. We will recall that the core of Jacotot's pedagogical theory was not the suppression or "subversion" of mastery, but the dissociation of the place of the master—and, specifically, his will, his exacting of speech from the student who otherwise has contempt for himself—from the presumed possession of knowledge. The master is a master because he does not know. A magisterial ignorance is, instead, a kind of meta-knowledge, that is, a decision: intelligence is one. But Rancière insists, in reading Jacotot, that this single intelligence is not a collective one (much less a "general intellect"). That intelligence be dispersed among individuals is the very condition of equality; equality is what must be appropriated, each time, over and over again. What is proposed in the displacement toward the "social effects" of emancipation is also a confrontation between two wills, and one intelligence: the will of the plebeians imposes a reconfiguration of the sensible, it makes it self-evident and undeniable that there is only one speech, one reason, polemically shared out between opposed social forces.

If we recall the specific situation of the emancipatory scene in Jacotot, the slumbering capacity of the student must be awakened by a type of vanguard, that is, a master or someone holding the place of the master who has *already* been emancipated. This emancipation, again, does not take the form of a prior possession of knowledge, but a prior demonstration of the capacity for anyone at all to verify, in a disciplined process, the sameness of the intellect.

The movement from individual emancipation to the constitution of a polemical space that is collective in nature effaces, then, the differences internal to the plebeian forces arrayed on the Aventine, or in the streets of Paris for that matter. What the difference between wills in the pedagogical scene made room for was the application of one will upon another. It left room, it left a place for the master. This place is swallowed up in the space of politics.

What would be the place of the master in politics? In other words, under the interrogation of what "intractable master" would the plebeians of ancient Rome have begun the disciplined process of demonstrating the oneness of intelligence, the axiom of equality? Clearly, the place of the master in the revolutionary tradition produced by the confluence of the workers' movement and Marxism was occupied by the problem of organization, by the need to bring together the strategic analysis of a theoretical knowledge or science with the already existing initiatives and struggles of the workers' movement. And if we were to separate, as does Jacotot, the place of the master from the possession of knowledge? What is projected in this thought experiment are perhaps the outlines of a new logic of organization, whose fundamental ambition and task is not the strategic guidance of the revolutionary forces latent in society and in the production process, but the cultivation of the *will* of the dominated, that is, a certain attention to their own powers and capacities, and a refusal to allow those powers to be forgotten, or this attention to be replaced with the self-contempt that is the condition of domination, the fertile soil of consensus.

THE MASTER IN HIS PLACE

[1] See, for example, Peter Hallward's excellent critical account of Rancière's oeuvre, "Jacques Rancière and the Subversion of Mastery," *Paragraph* 28:1 (2005): 26-45.

[2] I am referring, of course, to Jo Freeman's well-known 1974 essay by the same name, which is widely available online.

[3] Rancière, *The Ignorant Schoolmaster*, trans. Kristin Ross (Stanford: Stanford University Press, 1991), 38.

[4] Ibid., 13.

[5] Ibid., 38.

[6] Ibid., 17

[7] This is how Rancière describes the monastic community of brothers in "La communauté des egaux," in Jacques Rancière, *Aux bords du politique* (Paris: Gallimard, 1998), 141-48. All translations from this text are my own.

[8] Ibid., 14, 12.

[9] Ibid., 12.

[10] Ibid., 57, 54.

[11] Whatever their superficial similarities, we should be wary of identifying this mode of demanding speech from the student from the form of power isolated by Foucault in his refutation of the "repressive hypothesis," where power is said to be exercised not by means an interdiction of speech, but through its extraction.

[12] *The Ignorant Schoolmaster*, 29.

[13] Ibid., 79.

[14] Ibid., 80.

[15] Ibid., 21.

[16] *Aux bords du politique*, 84.

[17] *The Ignorant Schoolmaster*, 82.

[18] Ibid.

[19] Ibid., 98.

[20] Ibid., 31.

[21] Ibid., 108.

[22] Ibid., 102.

[23] Ibid., 105.

[24] Ibid., 82.

[25] Ibid., 2.

[26] *Aux bords du politique*, 160.

[27] *The Ignorant Schoolmaster*, 12.

[28] *Aux bords du politique*, 164.

[29] Ibid., 167.

[30] Ibid., 166-67

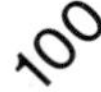

7

HOW IT IS WE REMAIN BARBARIAN

Evan Calder Williams

As those invested in Rancière's enterprise know, Schiller is at once a launching point and a sore spot, the conservative basis from which the attempt to make otherwise must depart. The success of such a recuperative operation is not the concern here. Rather, it is to offer a reading of Schiller that might bear on, or give different bearing to, the central problems of aesthetic education taken up by Rancière. For despite recognizing the specificity of Schiller's political stance and the material conditions against which such a stance was honed, neither establishing a more "faithful" reading of Schiller nor discarding whole hog the structure and terms of his thinking seems particularly useful in this regard. Instead, this is a historical updating of sorts, a dislocation, perhaps even a necessary one. After all, the general state of affairs Schiller discerned as a fresh wound to be closed, to be bridged by the playful zigzag stitches of the aesthetic, has become the bloodless and unhealed gash of the past two centuries. It simply is the case and nothing more. Such a shift cannot go unaccounted. To read him with a degree of generosity, then, or with a desire to have that reading mean more than curiosity, must be to read him against the letter of the text.

As a way to approach a Schiller who likely would not recognize himself (*shit, am I an anti-state communist?*), let's start with something right on the surface: Schiller the Catastrophist Pessimist, edging close to Schlegel's darker tint of gloom.

> Thus do we see the spirit of the age wavering between
> perversity and brutality, between unnaturalness and mere
> nature, between superstition and moral unbelief; and it
> is only through an equilibrium of evils that is still some-
> times kept within bounds.[1]

Two things worry Schiller, to put it mildly. Broadly speaking, we can think of them as the Natural State (or State of Nature or simply "Nature") and the Constructed State (within which we

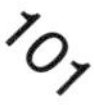

should include both his comments on "Civilization" as such and, in a more restricted register, on the European state-form proper.) The former, the Natural State, is impervious to moral condemnation. Defined not by a specific set of biological and geological qualities but by that which exists independent ("mere nature") of the volition or reason of man, it simply is, and it is "brutal." Pre-moral and pre-rational, the formal urges of Reason must aim to cloak it in the guise of decision.

> The force of his needs threw him into this situation
> before he was as yet capable of exercising his freedom to
> choose it; compulsion organized it according to purely
> natural laws before he could do so according to the laws
> of Reason.[2]

Hence, even if one would make the reasoned choice to accept the situation and terms of the Natural State, such a choice is not forthcoming. One is thrown into the aftermath of that compelled decision before choosing it to be the case. It is a choice that is made, indeed, to the degree that its conditions are retroactively accepted or struggled against (therein the emergence of a moral and ethical register), but one into which we were born all the same. Certain choices with this character should come immediately to mind, despite an apparent estrangement from any originary natural order. Choices, that is, like the much-vaunted "free sale of one's labor-power."

It is one thing to flatly assert a fundamental divide between the Natural State and the Constructed State, the former a bedrock to be alternately held at bay, reinforced, modulated, or chipped away by the latter. After all, such is the grounding move of almost all political theory. And to a degree, it remains Schiller's: the aesthetic thereby provides a key lability and mediation able to work through this divide and map its contours. Yet there is something highly particular about the structure of the Constructed State as fleshed out by Schiller.

> But what makes him Man is precisely this: that he does
> not stop short at what Nature herself made of him, but
> has the power of retracing by means of Reason the steps
> she took on his behalf, of transforming the work of blind
> compulsion into a work of free choice, and of elevating
> physical necessity.[3]

The initial specificity of the Constructed State—indeed, the very hydroplane of Civilization—is not its distance from Nature but its capacity for and tendency toward intense proximity. It hews faithfully to the given, not in order to transform its basic material arrangement but to swap out the formal sign under which it falls. It is the move from the necessity of physical law, as determinant of species-being, to the free necessity of the reasoned will, such that species-being ("what makes him Man") is the freedom to make a choice of what had never been. Therein lies the specificity of Schiller's "perversity," or at least the perversity he detects in the species: the unnatural act of miming nature before claiming it a triumph of the will. *Yes, we don't have much choice in the matter, but at least we chose it to be so!*

The material difference between a "passive" necessary order and an "active" contingent order that asserts itself by rationalizing and reproducing that necessity may be slight indeed, and claims of freedom are cold comfort to persistent degradation and misery. Nevertheless, it obtains as a rhetorical and categorical opposition, an axis around which Schiller's thought turns. It is the minimal difference that grounds the distance between *Stofftrieb* (material/sensuous drive) and *Formtrieb* (formal drive) and which consequently necessitates the *Spieltrieb* (play drive), the very engine bolstered and put to work by a program of aesthetic education.

However, it is here, on this initial point, that a historical retrofitting is needed, in order to read Schiller against both himself and the grain of common readings, in order to find the darker, nastier, scared, doubtful, and correct side of his thought. The updating derives from a basic fact: that entire mess of human constructions —above all the social relations of property and value, the built world, and the political mechanisms that are their joint protectorate—is neither structured nor experienced as a contingent construction. Nor is it as a work of materially-embedded reason within which volition, let alone "free choice," plays any significant role. They assert themselves, and are lived, as natural, as the very given to which Man can choose only to apply reason as an ornamental gilding of the non-compulsory. In short, we cannot understand the tendencies or limits of the "Constructed" as constructed. Furthermore, we exist in an order in which the divide between the ceaseless drive to create matter and the vicious imposition of forms upon the genesis and shaping of that matter can no longer be maintained. Such a division does not hold, either in the individual labor of those who exchange their days for wages or in the gargantuan currents of the world market. The material forms of what is built, sold, circulated, bought, and cast away cannot be parsed out. Our age does not waver in its spirit: it scrambles its poles.

This is an obvious and well-trod point. Anyone sentient knows how it feels. But it should not be reduced to a question of perspective, according to which we could strip away capital's self-same realism by being better historians. For while we should be better historians, that injunction ignores the fact that capital demands, posits, and brutally reinforces its status as Second Nature in ways that have nothing to do with the misprisions of category error. There's a danger on the other side, of falling into single trajectory narratives—for example, an irreversible and general slide toward the real subsumption of labor—which leave out the massive quantity of "non-economic" emergency measures needed to make it tick. Nevertheless, any account of capital's extension and development, from Schiller's time to ours, has to register a real shift in direction: from a period in which one could non-idiotically venture a position such as Schiller's, that framed the State of Nature and the Constructed State as it did, to the current moment, in which such an opposition is incoherent, irrelevant, and all too common, a vicious apology for a wracked and wrecking order.

The simple operation proposed, then, is to transpose Schiller's thought to the situation these days through a quite literal substitution: when he writes of "the State of Nature," read instead "capital" (or, for the sake of consistency, "the State of Second Nature"), taken broadly as the full and unsteady dominance of capital as the universal set of material relations. And conversely, when he speaks of the labor of reason, will, progress, Civilization, and the State, read instead the range of contemporary attempts to alternately manage, sustain, exacerbate, or, most rarely, sever the trends and contradictions of naturalized capital.

(The second substitution is less dramatic, but it seems necessarily so, as we should resist the urge to enact a full flipping of terms, suspicion of facile inversion aside. It would be simply wrong to understand the structural position of the Constructed State in Schiller's thought as analogous to that of the State of Nature, that pastoral phantom, these days. Rather, the task is to grasp that the attempts to retrace by reason and to give form anew take as their terrain the material and social landscape of capital, as something unreasonable and non-negotiable. In such a situation, any idea of "Nature as such," both as a set of material resources and limits indifferent to what we might like to do with them and as a determinant concept without which we can't think trends of development and management, cannot be easily situated in the opposition motivating Schiller's thought. It is a properly messy split, including at once a subtending condition always threatening to rear its head, a pure fantasy reserve of green nostalgia and liquids that can burn well, and a negative definition that persists, particularly in times when the contradictions of capital bare themselves with an elevated degree of viciousness.)

Artificial reading project as this is, it is not a textual game. It's an attempt to know Schiller as one who was historically specific about the time in which he wrote and to see if that thought still bears on what is, without question, a drastically different historical landscape. The gambit is, first, that an under-remarked and compelling other side of Schiller might come to light, of which this fundamental shift from State of Nature to State of Second Nature is a key part, and second, that it might give a different angle of inflection to questions bearing the name *aesthetic education*.

Regarding the first: insofar as another Schiller comes to light, it is a very dark one. He is full of spite, doubt, and bile, all of which was there from the start but which was previously restrained and tempered by the relative stability of the oppositions—between Nature and Civilization, between given and built, and between sensuous and formal—without which the aesthetic, as mediation and transition, could not obtain. Consider the following, with substitution indicated:

> When the craftsman has a timepiece to repair, he can let
> its wheels run down; but the living clockwork of the State
> [representational politics and its material supports] must
> be repaired while it is still striking, and it is a question of
> changing the revolving wheel while it still revolves. For
> this reason a support must be looked for which will ensure
> the continuance of society, and make it independent of the
> Natural State [Capital] which is to be abolished.[4]

Aside from the petty frisson of reworking Schiller such that he speaks of support mechanisms that exceed the abolition of capital, there is a real difference at hand, in degree if not in kind. In the *Letters*, Schiller's doubt about, and horror in the possible face of, the success of revolutions does not interrogate their form. He is speaking properly about revolutions—bourgeois ones, at that—rather than insurrections, about "changing the revolving wheel" without disrupting its revolution, sticking something in its spokes, or, God forbid, questioning if the shape of the wheel or the axle itself might not dictate the kind of forward movement to follow the repair. However, rereading Schiller as proposed brings out a latent element in his work that proves crucial: namely, *a defense of separation*. Even insofar as his aesthetics, and Rancière's initial inheritance from him, functions precisely by means of a crossing or blurring, and therefore constitutes a practical critique of the logic of separation it cannot do without it. (In more ways than one, we can understand the project of Rancière's aesthetics as fixated on this question, from the concern to undo the opposition of theatrical activity and spectacular passivity to claims of the collapse of a distinct partition of the sensible that previously designated artistic experience. His thought works out a continuation of this model in that it takes on as its determinant source a theoretical impasse to be reworked.) In terms of the aesthetics, this means that the unifying movement of the *Spieltrieb* is not just a response to the gulf between the sensuous and the formal. It is that which *reinforces* that divide and insists on a distance that exists to be crossed. In that it claims to elaborate the play between matter and form, it necessarily asserts that one can tell the difference to start with, that there is a salient distinction between the construction of the sensuous and the abstraction from it, and, ultimately, that such a difference involves an opposition between the thoughtless production of Nature (even as a realm of unwilled human activity) and the reasoned production of Man (even as a tracing or approximation of inhuman morphologies).

It's no surprise, then, that the prospect of the collapse of separation is not, for Schiller, a jubilant moment, not even a generative unbinding. It is the site of his greatest pessimism, as he confronts a worsening that lacks defined coasts of judgment and renounces not the aesthetic as such, but the primary splitting on which any future shuttling back and forth of sense depends. This problem is indexed most precisely by the status of revolutions and the unfathomable difficulty of starting otherwise. If seen as near impossible, or at least not worth all those red-slicked streets and blown opportunities in his period, a present Schiller would find the blacker suspicions confirmed. Not merely of the practical absence of a support mechanism to outlast the end of the given. Worse, the inability to develop any such mechanism of transition not beholden to the logic of the order whose abolition it stewards.

Can we perhaps look for such action from the State?
That is out of the question. For the State as at present

constituted has been the cause of the evil, while the State
as Reason conceives it, far from being able to lay the
foundations of this better humanity, would itself have to
be founded on it.[5]

Even without a transposition to present conditions, this is a more summary and correct dispatching of reformism than the vast majority of communist and anarchist thinkers have ever pulled off. In short, one has two non-options: either this bourgeois State, which is the continued imposition of the hell of Second Nature and hence cannot swerve from its determined path, or an other state ("as Reason conceives it," i.e. a speculative venture) which could only be a consequence of an order yet to come. The former is merely more of the same, and the latter is impossible to explain, envisioning the State as an retroactive evental emergence beamed back from the better humanity (a Third Nature?) which it needs to break the deadlock of the already given. When one fully takes on the contemporary fact that both given and constructed belong to the same order of capital's materially-embedded formal relations, the severity of the impasse becomes all the starker. Schiller, conservative as he was, appears to have sniffed it out better than most.[6]

What Schiller's thought marks is a time in which both the deadlock of starting over and the confusion of the natural-constructed opposition become visible, precisely in that they become extraordinarily hard to parse out or untangle. The aesthetic, then, is the name given to what might, and won't, dodge this, what might track a way out of the static and fog.

One stands in a moment of sloppy catastrophe, in which

> The fabric of the natural State [read: Capital] is tottering,
> its rotting foundations giving way, and there seems to be
> a physical possibility of setting law upon the throne, of
> honouring man at last as an end in himself, and making
> true freedom the basis of political associations. Vain hope!
> The moral possibility is lacking, and a moment so prodigal
> of opportunity finds a generation unprepared to receive it.[7]

Yet the passage from Schiller's moment to one in which such a gulf—between a tottering natural state and an inadequate labor of reason—no longer obtains is not a minor one. It's not merely an augmentation of the massive, spiteful doubt ("Vain hope!") made all the more pressing by a good two centuries of rotting foundations.

The critique of separation has not lost its urgency, but it has lost the clarity of the separated. And so, a different approach to that same decaying material is needed, not a negative aesthetics but one doesn't start from the recurrent failure of the attempt to "set law upon the throne." In other words, you don't *need* aesthetics because an Enlightenment project of rational governance didn't work out. Our question would be better framed by Schiller's suspicion about the general capacity to start otherwise, rather than the accidents of those who may or may not be morally ready to receive them.

In short, it's not about how to dodge a catastrophe by correctly receiving an opportunity to enthrone reason: it's how you receive a catastrophe correctly, taking it on not as a disaster waiting in the wings, but as a basic compass bearing. How do you receive such a disaster in such a way, as the means and at the moment of seizing, to obliterate those morals, that law, that throne, and that very attempt to gain its position? How do you neither intervene in such a way that merely reestablishes an increasingly hobbled and anxious rule of law nor not intervene, such that a blurring of separation would be left to slur into a truly incoherent mess? Difficult as it is to fathom or elaborate in its concrete particulars, it would be a reception that abolishes as it takes up: such is the only cogent response to what is already rotting under foot and overhead. Certainly not to pile fresh timber on the termites…

As the phrasing here indicates, I am evoking two registers and theoretical traditions, one "political" and one "aesthetic." First, a long-standing but contentious communist line of thinking about the way in which working class struggles reproduce the very category of the working class, hence the necessity of the proletariat not seizing the upper hand—not "taking power"—but abolishing itself as a class and rupturing the social relation of capital. In short, a problem about the historical incompatibility of a material force (the working class) and an evolving form (value) that would be wrecked by severing the relation without which neither makes any sense. Second, a sense of the aesthetic not necessarily as the harmonious interplay of formal and material drives but as that which categorically registers the ever-collapsing space between them, which begins at breakdown and stays there. In short, a highly fraught mapping of that recognizably political problem of historical incompatibility.

And so, if aesthetics, as a line of inquiry, remains of import to political thought, it might have very little to do with either a realm of free play that models harmony or what could interrogate, to take a common example, the conditions of visibility within which political subjects appear. Instead, it is what is located exactly on the axis of the problem that bears the name *politics*. It demonstrates, more specifically, the frozen decomposition and the perspectival decoherence of that problem. This is crucial, though, because the fall-out of these problems—the extraction into a different register ("aesthetics") and the emergence of properties ("aesthetic") divorced from the general system in which it makes sense—generates some breathing and thinking room. A rather obvious reason for this is that the material and form in question can be not *just* "masses of rioters" and "the historical forms of non-state organization" but "thick red" and "the historical forms of color field painting." Yet such a perspective might open more widely onto the traditional objects of aesthetic experience or inquiry, i.e. objects that get themselves called *art*. In very brief, it starts to point a way past the recurrent problem of the profound shittiness of the vast majority of "political art": that which attempts to transpose a set of political concerns into the sphere of aesthetic education and experience, and, more often than not, vice versa (see here: "street theater," "zombie bankers," "peaceful marches"). Insofar as the aesthetic marks not a sphere of experience in which politics *could* appear but the rather specialized zone that is founded on shared impasses, even as it is perhaps "supposed" to temper them, we see that a) it is ultimately marked off less by standing in uneasy opposition to "life"[8] than to the prospect of any real clarity and duration of sustained relations themselves (i.e. aesthetics becomes the name not of the delimited zone with its own properties but of the extraordinary difficulty of delimiting much at all, of parsing out form and matter, choice and determination).

But even if one of the more basic negative indications of what would fall under aesthetic inquiry—art as not-life, at least not until "after the revolution"!—does not especially hold water, the question is different when we speak of aesthetic *education*. For on that terrain, we are indeed speaking of *lives*, of people and subjects who could potentially gain or lose something, as bourgeois citizens or as torch-bearing proles. And while the question of the unstable separation marked jointly by the end of politics and the start of aesthetics is distinctly posed against specific subjects remaining what they are through a process, aesthetic education focuses on exactly that, even as it can point beyond it.

With this emerges an immediate problem: what if the subjects at hand are genuinely incapable—or unwilling—of participating in such a process, no matter how non-hierarchical or posed against the transmission of master knowledge it may be? What if they are not ignorant but *stupid*, not lacking but unfocused? What if they are so both *in general* and *in particular*? And what if they are not merely uninterested but hateful?

I guard this intentionally old-fashioned language of stupidity and the "they to be educated" to both note a recurrent problem in the discourse of aesthetic education from Schiller on and to insist that there is something that should not be tossed out in the seemingly offensive bathwater. In moving toward an ending, I consider how Schiller poses these questions and gesture toward their continuation as lines of inquiry deserving further thought.

The bleaker Schiller of our investigation reveals another striking angle of doubt about transformative processes: namely, the perversity and brutality of the age do not signal a distance from a coherent and lost "complete man" there to be rediscovered. Rather,

> the image of the human species is projected in magnified form into separate individuals—but as fragments, not in different combinations, with the result that one has to go the rounds from one individual to another in order to be able to piece together a complete image of the species.[9]

In other words, if there is a non-perverse species-being to return to, it is perversely common yet scattered out amongst people in an anthropological equivalent of the specialization of labor. And so, "man himself develops into nothing but a fragment"; he "becomes nothing more than the imprint of his occupation or of his specialized knowledge."[10] This is bad enough, given that it produces the same problem of founding a new State off the extant ruins of the present one. But it gets worse: "We see not merely individuals, but whole classes of men, developing but one part of their potentialities, while of the rest, as in stunted growths, only vestigial traces remain."[11] That is, the degradation from species-being ("the image of the human species" as lived particularly) to *specific being* is neither a passive slide nor is it evenly distributed across the species, such that "everyone has something special to offer" or anything of the kind. All are fragmented, but while some get the chance to at least bring out—to *educate*—what remains in an approximation of being Man, others are restricted to the education of *one aspect* of their species (hint: capacity to produce value), if at all. This is, after all, a theory of class, of the misallocation of sensibility and potential.

Following from this, a reorientation of aesthetic education might be in order, one that shifts it from *ignorance*—Rancière's particular emphasis—to *stupidity*, which hangs around the edges of our pessimist Schiller. Ignorance marks a state of a *lack* of knowledge, even in the retrofitted conception ventured by Rancière, that could be addressed, supplemented, or overcome by a program: one can know that one does not know, and the realization of not knowing is the overcoming of ignorance. No such luck with stupidity. Derived from *stupere* ("to be struck, stunned, amazed"), stupidity indicates two key things. First, a fundamental violence. It is a battering into stupidity, a crushing down to incoherence. It is not a state of knowledge that can be overcome but a state of being, the consequence of a material situation that acts upon you. Second, a temporary state of being. Unlike idiocy,[12] one is not stupid as such. One can be stupid, but it marks a limited period of time in which that is one's condition. It may last a long time, but it is the consequence, above all, of a set of external conditions, not an internal failure or need, that reduce one, or many, to the state of inertia, dullness, insensitivity, and stasis. When we are stupid, crucially, *we cannot be educated, by ourselves or others.* It is the fundamental state of non-reception, sparkless, without curiosity, too beaten into non-receptivity.

To take this on gestures toward two important questions. First, if the specificity of aesthetic education is the development of judgment and the augmentation of capacities through aesthetic experience, and if the temporary closure that is stupidity acts as the fundamental threat to this that must be warded off, what of aesthetic experiences that produce stupidity? That batter us, not into a shock of the estranging new, but into a sludge of non-thought?[13] Second, and more importantly, what of *distraction*? Distraction is itself one of the main threats to education, institutional or self-directed: the constant loss of focus, the buzzing anxiety of attention scattered out into a constant stream of useless efforts. Yet if we shift our register away from ignorance toward stupidity—the historical stupidity of class, of those "insensate" to aesthetic experience because of an "education" in the violence and tedium of labor—as the grounding threat and condition, distraction takes on a different character. It becomes less the characteristic to be disciplined or reined in and more the critical movement that signals the restarting of thought. It is the first stirring of sense out from beneath the weight of stupidity, that which declares, in its furtive sneaking of sight and mind away from the task at hand, that the available options are boring, mediocre, and incapable of effecting any change. It rejects the particular incarnation of education that hinges on *development* and *program* by the very fact that distraction thinks diagonally, leaving what is materially at hand for what is imaginatively exciting (the daydream) or vice versa, dropping flights of abstraction for what hands can do now (fidgeting, doodling, vandalizing). This shouldn't be transposed into a flat rejection of the role of education, a deeply boring move itself. Rather, the questions on which it bears are, in a properly distracted shift of register, aesthetic and political. To what degree does the very instability of the aesthetic depend, fundamentally, on the distraction of thought, slipping restlessly back and forth between form and matter? And to what degree does distraction mark a necessary departure from political programs, from those that expect attention and focus, that expect subjects to behave themselves at rallies and stay on task, that think consciousness is something to be "raised"? From those who insist that a correct optic should restrict our attention to what clearly appears as correctly and identifiably political, rather than to the profound strangeness—*Why are they still in the streets when they have "won their demands"? Why is no one leading this march? Why are they looting sneakers? Why are firefighters killing cops?*—that actually indicates an insurrectionary turn? What would it mean to build up a disciplined distraction?

If stupidity and distraction have to do with an unbidden state of present affairs (one doesn't choose to get stupid, and it's highly difficult to focus on being distracted), another line to follow, and with which to end, is that of the choice to reject the present's options in full. For Schiller, this is marked by the prospect of being "at odds with oneself," described below with our modifications:

> But man can be at odds with himself in two ways: either as a savage, when feeling predominates over principle; or as barbarian, when principle destroys feeling. The savage despises Civilization [the construction of the community], and acknowledges Nature as his sovereign mistress. The barbarian derides and dishonours Nature [Capital], but, more contemptible than the savage, as often as not continues to be the slave of his slave.[14]

It is the barbarian that interests us. It stands not just as a convenient figure of this hatred but as a key problem of aesthetic education in an era of admixture, blurring, and the crisis of the aesthetic (as discernible sphere and as the particular anxiety of separation it has always noted). For while the savage is clear enough (ignorant, with a flat love of Nature, for reasons of unquestioned adherence to the given, and a consequent hatred of attempts to build anew), the barbarian remains opaque, in Schiller's text and elsewhere, as a long-standing marker of what is incompatible with a social order. Because, crucially, Schiller does not state that the barbarian therefore loves civilization or acknowledges its mastery: principle and civilization are not equivalent, although the text sets them up as such. What can be glimpsed here, then, is a *barbarian principle*, one that admits its own stupidity, as the very reason why it hates the given. It is a principle not identical to the mimetic work of reason that feebly imitates, or barely deviates from, the laws of the given, yet with which one can have accord. It is a prospect of holding one's own by holding to a line that belongs neither to the accepted nor the proposed, neither to the individual fragment nor to the reproduction of class. Such a line, it seems, is precisely the darker version of aesthetics elaborated here, which believes neither in nature nor construction but only in following the unraveling thread that once stitched between them.

Because, after all, to say that the barbarian "as often as not continues to be the slave of his slave" is to say that there are instances, however "not often," in which this deriding and disdaining actually obtains. Those, it seems, are our instances, when such a hate takes. Such a hate is difficult. It must be tended and stoked and built. It deserves, perhaps, the education it loathes and ignores, the aesthetic knots it tries to cut bluntly. And more often than not we remain the same, beaten, worsened, and more stupid than ever. But still, there is that "as not." How to make something of that? That is a barbarian's question. It is still the pressing one.

<hr>

[1] Friedrich Schiller, *On the Aesthetic Education of Man*, trans. Elizabeth M. Wilkinson and L.A. Willoughby (Oxford: Oxford University Press, 1983), 29. Such an honest appraisal of one's time, incorrect as it may be as to the "source" of this spirit's determination, remains a real bracing tonic these days.

[2] Ibid., 13; my emphasis.

[3] Ibid.

[4] Ibid.

[5] Ibid., 45.

[6] Like other great conservative thinkers (such as Juan Donoso Cortés), he at least does us the favor of openly baring his doubt about the plausibility of a conservative enterprise, far more than liberals have ever done. We see as well the specificity of the classical conservative stance, which tends to argue from the worst-case scenario in order to render all normal functions of the state as emergency measures. The State, therefore, must dominate and intervene at all moments in order to prevent the slide through that tiny degree of worsening into the normal conditions of life as such: brutality, criminality, brevity. Meanwhile, it performs the same operation in reverse, normalizing emergency measures (capital punishment, war, martial law) as business as usual and therefore not a threat to the story that the State intervenes as little as in the lives and affairs of its population.

[7] Schiller, *On the Aesthetic Education of Man*, 25.

[8] Rancière himself has done a lot of work in trying to trouble this old-school inadequate pairing, albeit one which has been quite determinant through incorporation into both theoretical and artistic practice. In one of his sharper one-liners: "There is no opposition between life and mausoleum"... (*Dissensus*, trans. Steve Corcoran [London: Continuum, 2010], 122.)

[9] Schiller, *On the Aesthetic Education of Man*, 33.

[10] Ibid., 35.

[11] Ibid., 33.

[12] The roots of idiocy as an existential and political category are deep ones: consider Plutarch's definition of the idiot as the one who is not a citizen.

[13] The discourse surrounding the sublime has traditionally indexed this, but with the prospect that, terror of evacuated cognitive faculties aside, it nevertheless expands judgment in the long run.

[14] Schiller, *On the Aesthetic Education of Man*, 21.

8

REALISM, DIS-IDENTIFICATION AND THE IMAGE

Maria Muhle

In his well-known book on the politics of aesthetics, *The Distribution of the Sensible,* Jacques Rancière localizes the "aesthetic revolution," i.e. the passage from the representative to the aesthetic regime of the arts, in the forms of literary realism. And he explains that these forms of realism do not obey the imperative of resemblance, but rather are to be understood as a negation or suspension of the classical hierarchies of representation—hierarchies Rancière summarizes with the Aristotelian use of the term "mimesis" that designates a normative aesthetics of genres. Rancière's realism, which I would like to call an "aesthetic realism," is thus a post-mimetic, post-representative form of representation, and this means in the first place that it does not aim at an authentic reproduction of reality (it is thus situated beyond the classical tradition's imperative of resemblance), and, in the second place, that it establishes a general representability of all subject matter beyond the hierarchies of representation that regulate what (subject matter) can be shown, in which way (in a serious, comical, emphatic, etc., way), and on which support (on a canvas, a photography, a stage, or in a museum).

At the same time, it is also important not to forget that this transition from the representative to the aesthetic regime of the arts, as Rancière recalls, does not coincide with the transition from a modern to a post-modern age in the aesthetics, nor does the end of the representative regime give way to a modernist "end of representation," i.e. abstraction and the proclamation of art's autonomy. Instead, as I have pointed out, what is at stake in this transition or rupture is a special form of post-representative and post-normative realism: "The leap outside of *mimesis* is by no means the refusal of figurative representation. Furthermore its inaugural moment has often been called realism, which does not in any way mean the valorization of resemblance but rather the destruction of the structures within which it functioned. Thus, novelistic realism is first of all the reversal of hierarchies of representation (the primacy of the narrative over the descriptive or the hierarchy of subject matter) and the adoption of a fragmented or proximate mode of focalization, which imposes raw presence to the detriment of the rational sequences of the story."[1]

In what follows, I will take this affirmation of a "reversal of hierarchies of representation" seriously and examine its function within the framework of Jacques Rancière's political aesthetics. In order to do so, I will start with an account of the so-called historical "origin" of pictorial realism in the 19th century that already features, as I will show, the fundamental ambiguity of the notion of realism. In a second step, I will then draw on more contemporary forms of realist (or documentary) images, the films of the Medvedkin Group, that reflect this ambiguity and the struggle around (aesthetic and political) representation. As an open conclusion, I would like to present an artistic strategy, Asier Mendizabal's work *Cinema* (1999), which establishes a scene where this struggle over images is introduced in an archive of self-representational strategies and becomes addressable as such.

Mechanical reproduction

In his "Little History of Photography," Walter Benjamin quotes a critical commentary by Charles Baudelaire on the photographic revolution: "In these sorry days, a new industry has arisen that has done not a little to strengthen the asinine belief … that art is and can be nothing other than the accurate reflection of nature … A vengeful god has hearkened to the voice of this multitude. Daguerre is his messiah."[2] Baudelaire also comments in a similar way on realism in painting, and especially so on the painting of his friend Gustave Courbet, who he accuses of a "lack of imagination," since he legitimizes his art through the imitation of an external model and therefore finally subordinates it to that very mechanistic paradigm that necessarily, following Baudelaire, is the contradiction or the end of art. Baudelaire's criticism of photographic *and* pictorial realism is thus symptomatic of the dispute with realism because it describes the production of mimetic resemblance (be it pictorial or photographic) as a mechanistic or automatic reproduction of reality, and therefore as necessarily non-artistic.

On the contrary, the so-called "realists"—the term was first used in a negative way to criticize the new ways of painting and/ or writing and was then appropriated by Gustave Courbet and his friend and writer Jules Champfleury, for example—use the notion of realism precisely to call into question this division between art and non-art, the creative and the purely mechanical and focus their concerns on the subject matter of representation: the reality that is to be represented without omitting any disturbing, unsettling or "ugly" detail, without beautifying the social context it reflects.[3] In his *Realist Manifesto* from 1855, Courbet defines the aim of his realist painting as "to translate the customs, the ideas, the appearance of my epoch according to my own appreciation," rather than following the aesthetic norms that regulate representation. Courbet's art claims to consider all appearances of the visible world as equally worth depicting. In this sense, continues Courbet, realism is "in its essence a democratic art." Or, in Champfleury's words commenting on the protest against Courbet's "Stone Breakers" (1849), exhibited in the 1850-51 *Salon de Peinture* in Paris: "People could not admit that a stone breaker was worth as much as a prince: the nobility objected to him according so many meters of canvas to ordinary people; only sovereigns had the right to be painted full length, with their decorations, their rich clothes and their official expressions. No one wants to admit that a stonebreaker is equal to a prince. The nobility is filled with indignation about the fact that just as much canvas is used for the little people. Only the sovereign has the right to be represented in full figure...."[4]

Around the same time, the French novelist Gustave Flaubert writes that his novel *Madame Bovary* (1857), the paradigmatic example of French realism and of "democracy in literature," had been written "in hatred of realism [*en haine du réalisme*]." He permanently complains about the vulgarity of his subject matter,[5] which obliges him, as Erich Auerbach puts it, to "tiresome stylistic meticulousness" or in Flaubert's own words: *dire à la fois simplement et proprement des choses vulgaires*.[6] Even though Flaubert ironically complains about the formal consequences of his choice of subject matter, he fully engages with the main aspect of realism, as exposed by both Courbet and Champfleury, and later theorized by Auerbach, namely "the serious treatment of everyday reality."[7]

To summarize, one could say that Baudelaire reduces realism to a strictly mimetic or mechanical representation, understood as the exact imitation and reproduction of reality or of nature, which he condemns because it dangerously reduces the creative power of art to mechanical reproduction—a move that heralds the end of art. Flaubert, for his part, does not even bother to criticize this "representative" notion of realism, but goes, unlike Baudelaire, beyond the limitations of its indexical character by putting forward or operating with a wider notion of realism, in which representation is not subjected to the rule of semblance and verisimilitude, but is grounded instead on the indifference of its subject matter. Flaubert thus agrees with Courbet in considering realism a rupture with the rules or conventions of representation, which traditionally exclude specific objects—for example, stonebreakers or provincial housewives—from serious or "sublime" (Auerbach) representation because of their unworthiness: a stonebreaker is materially speaking not worth the canvas he is being represented on, and he is therefore not worthy of being "in art." The formal critique of realism as mechanization of artistic creation is therefore accompanied by the critique of the content of representation: the everyday, the poor, the masses, or provincial housewives and their boredom.

What is especially interesting is the examination of how this twofold critique is transposed to the discussion of mechanical image production par excellence, photography, and how it unveils, if we follow Benjamin, a necessary relation between the technical apparatus and the rupture with a traditional scheme of representation: it is therefore not the discussion about the necessary or contingent, the possible or impossible objective representation of reality that constitutes the technical innovation of photography, but rather the possibility of representing everything, be it a larger number of people, unimportant details, accidental subjects, etc. The "unimportant detail" or the nameless person in the background of an image gain a specific status in the photographic picture, as opposed to the painting that always refers to the intention of the painter ("the pictures, if they last, do so only as testimony to the art of the painter"[8]). Not objectivity but general representability—the representation of something, "that goes beyond testimony to the photographer's art, something that cannot be silenced, that fills you with an unruly desire to know what her name was, the woman who was alive there, who even now is still real and will never consent to be wholly absorbed in 'art'"[9]: the representation of the Newhaven fishwife by Octavius Hill that paradigmatically stands for the arbitrariness, banality, and prosaicness of the subject matter of the new techniques is thus the main artifice of the mechanical image.

Aesthetic Realism

To recapitulate, we could say that the forms of aesthetic realism are thus defined by two intertwined conditions: they no longer obey the imperative of resemblance or authentic or objective representation (they are therefore a post-authentic representation) and they establish a general representability of all subject matter as equally important and meaningful (it is therefore a post-normative or post-representative representation).

But the forms of aesthetic realism not only bring visibility to the formerly invisible, representation to those below the threshold of representation, light to the darkness to paraphrase Brecht's dictum attributed by him to Mack the Knife. By disrupting the common norms of representation, they call into question the relation of representation as such insofar as they suspend the division between represented reality and real reality, i.e., they keep this relation undetermined or undecided. This keeping undecided enables a reflection on the general conditions under which reality can appear or be accessible in the first place, that is, a level on which divisions and classifications of realities are performed. The forms of aesthetic realism refer to this level. They are therefore not bound to image-theoretical norms of authenticity or indexicality, but instead understand them as norms of the representative regime that are no longer applicable in an aesthetic politics of representation: for these are predominantly characterized by grasping the relation of documentary and fictional depiction as an "uncertainty relation" as Hito Steyerl has recently called it,[10] meaning that the attributions of specific forms to specific subjects are interrupted—something that can be discerned in the large number of fictional-documentary works in recent years. Rancière articulates this "aesthetic revolution" with regard to Flaubert's literary realism as follows: "There are no longer appropriate subjects for art. As Flaubert puts it, 'Yvetot is as good as Constantinople' and the adulteries of a farmer's daughter are as good as those of Theseus, Oedipus or Clytemnestra. There are no longer rules of appropriateness between a particular subject and a particular form, but a general availability of all subjects for any artistic form whatsoever."[11]

Accordingly, reality—or politics for that matter—appears where there is resistance to any "representative" articulation of reality, in the suspension of the norms of representation. In this suspension, that which is suspended attains a strange status of reality that resists a determining approach – in image-theoretical terms: an authenticating or indexicalizing understanding/conception of reality —thus referring it to its potentiality, i.e., its ability to be shifted and altered. And according to Rancière, that is exactly what constitutes the political claim of artistic forms whose relation to the real do not simply indicate reality or continue and fix its constellations, but stage the contingency of the constitution of this reality and thus its changeability.

Dis-Identification

The politics that might take place in this disrupting of the normative relation that structures the common is therefore strictly opposed to the assumption of a binary division between those who have knowledge and are therefore aware of their conditions, and those who have neither knowledge nor consciousness, and depend therefore on the transmission of knowledge and the unveiling of the ideological structures their life is trapped within. In this sense, politics can no longer aim at enlightening those who don't know, or occupying the speaker's position to represent them. It must instead construct a place where those who traditionally, that is "naturally," are not supposed or allowed to be part of public life and thus of the construction of the common can claim a sensible appearance and therefore redistribute the contingent but existing distribution of shares. For Rancière, this redistribution of places, voices and times is a political one insofar as it actualizes what he calls an "axiomatic equality" or, famously in *The Ignorant Schoolmaster*, the "equality of intelligences"; and he describes this gesture as a figure of subjectivation, i.e. a "disidentification, a removal from the naturalness of a place, the opening up of a subject space where anyone can be counted since it is the space where those of no account are counted, where a connection is made between having a part and having no part,"[12] as he puts it in *Disagreement*.

Thus, the opposite of subjectivation is identification, that is, the police activity of assigning everybody its "natural" place and function. To undo the implementation of this "natural" order, subjectivation "repartitions the field of experience that gave to each other their identity with their lot."[13] Politics is thought of as the historical a priori conditions of the "perceptible organization" of the common—that is, as the conditions of possibility for people and/or things to appear as something else, to undo the "representative" articulation of reality.

This appearance is not simply the construction of a new identity that would give way to another partition of the common – or put plainly, it is not sheer visibility that constitutes the aesthetics of politics. Rather, the goal is the unsettling of identification itself:

Political appearance in the Rancièrian sense is about making a connection between having a part and having no part in the common, which means that the factual appearance of those who have no part does not lead to their integration into a democratic space of communication, but to a highlighting of the distribution of the sensible as a system of representation, that is, as a normative system that assigns activities and possibilities, visibility and sayability, to specific roles and places. The forms of aesthetic realism thus have a political claim, insofar as they destabilize this normative system of representation and fracture the traditional scheme of expectations, hierarchies and identifications.

Infamous Imitation

This strategy of aesthetic-political dis-identification is in a paradoxical way at work in what Foucault has described as the lives of infamous men, accessing a visibility through the excessive imitation of the rhetoric of sovereign power in the so-called "lettres de cachet." In the introduction to a compilation of texts that never appeared, "Lives of Infamous Men," Foucault points to the paradoxical detail that these existences are only brought to us ("into light") because of their accidental encounter with power: "What snatched them from the darkness in which they could, perhaps should, have remained was the encounter with power; without that collision, it's very unlikely that any word would be there to recall their fleeting trajectory."[14] For Foucault, these documents are "'fable[s]' of obscure lives, from which the fabulous was banned" and he indirectly approves of the Auerbachian rupture when he writes: "The impossible or the ridiculous ceased to be the condition under which the ordinary could be recounted. An art of language was born whose task was no longer to tell of the improbable but to bring into view that which doesn't, which can't and mustn't appear —to tell the last and most tenuous degrees of the real."[15] Thus, the new imperative of Western Literature, Foucault concludes, would be to search "for these things hardest to perceive—the most hidden, hardest to tell and show."[16]

In the Foucauldian approach, this imperative necessarily has its counterpart in the analysis of the Christian confession as a tool of pastoral power to penetrate these same lives in their totality and in every single detail. At the same time, I would like to stress that this penetration by power does not neutralize the unsettling effects these documents have on the very same logic of power, that they breached accidentally and unintentionally, but only confirms the necessary and double relation of literature (or the written word) "to truth and to power"[17]: they are part of a constellation of power-knowledge in which every movement produces a counter-movement, every discourse produces a counter-discourse that is not necessarily intentional or total, but that can also be accidental and fragmentary, as in the case of the infamous existences that survive in the administrative documents that were meant to ascribe them exclusively to one situation and position in society.

It is thus important to reformulate the question of the visibility of those who rather pathetically are called the "infamous," the "excluded," "minorities," etc., within the framework of an aesthetic realism in order to avoid the *topos* of the sheer "elevation" of the infamous through their inclusion in an established realm of the political (their upgrading to "worthy" subjects or to subjects tout court). In the following I would like to examine two films that address this problem of representation and self-representation in a very specific manner both in their subject matter, the representation of a worker's strike in Besançon in 1967 and 1968, and their form, or rather in their shift of forms, the shift from a reflexive to a self-reflexive documentary film that enacts the appropriation of the means of representation and thereby rejects an external view.

À bientôt, j'espère

In March 1967, Pol Cèbe and other members of the *Centre Culturel Populaire de Palente-les-Orchamps* (CCPPO) invited the Parisian filmmaker Chris Marker to follow the strike and the occupation of the production plant of Rhodiacéta, a textile branch of Rhône-Poulenc in Besançon. In collaboration with Mario Marret and the workers of Rhodiacéta, Marker produced the film *A bientôt, j'espère*, which documents the ongoing struggles, focusing on the strike that took place in February and March 1967, which was being ignored by the mainstream media. In his film, Marker highlights the fact that this is the first occupation of a factory in France since 1936, comments on its extended duration (it lasted for 26 days, from February 26 to March 24, 1967) and on the fact that it had spread quickly to other units of the corporation. The film aims to present this strike not as a singular event, but as part of a long list of social movements and strikes that cannot be understood, as the voice-over explains, as "an adding up of victories and defeats but as different steps in a struggle."

The opening scene of the film is at once emblematic for the documentary style adopted by Marker and the *"film-ouvrier,"* the "workers' film," for which *À bientôt, j'espère* is one of the first examples. We see one of the main actors of the social movement and of the film, Georges Maurivard, also known as Yoyo, union activist and worker at the Rhodiacéta, in front of the factory gates, trying to gather his co-workers to inform them about the dismissal of ninety-two workers in Lyon. It is a few days before Christmas, as the voice-over says, and thus months after the occupation and successful strike in February and March. The camera shows the workers leaving the factory (and gathering around the speaker) and so inevitably refers to the first scene ever shot in the history of cinema by the Lumière brothers, a 45-second sequence depicting workers at the photography factory in Lyon owned by the brothers themselves, hurrying out of the factory gates for lunch. In this way, the beginning of Marker's film comments at once on the construction of a political space and on a media event, i.e. the birth of cinema.[18]

More explicitly, Marker relates the factory gates to the very emergence of a "political culture" by documenting the events, by interviewing the main actors of the social movement, and by giving background and practical information about the factory as well as about the hovering threat of massive dismissals. The voice-over gives the necessary clues to understanding the strike and by doing so inscribes the film in a classical documentary paradigm, where the documentary images reflect reality and the voice-over explains this reality by situating it politically and historically.[19] Marker's voice comments on the images of March 1967, highlighting the originality of the strike, its length, and its form, and above all, "the idea, that has been continually taken up again, that the imbalance in the working conditions translates into an imbalance in life in its totality, which could not be compensated by a salary increase." He thus inscribes the strike in a broader political and ideological situation and defines its aim as the questioning of the very form of the Welfare State—and not integration into its society. Therefore, he concludes, the measure of its success is not first of all the increase in salaries but the "education of a whole new generation of workers through social conflict."

The traditional use of interviews also remains in this paradigm, when the workers answer the filmmaker's questions and give explanations of their situation and their path to militancy—for example

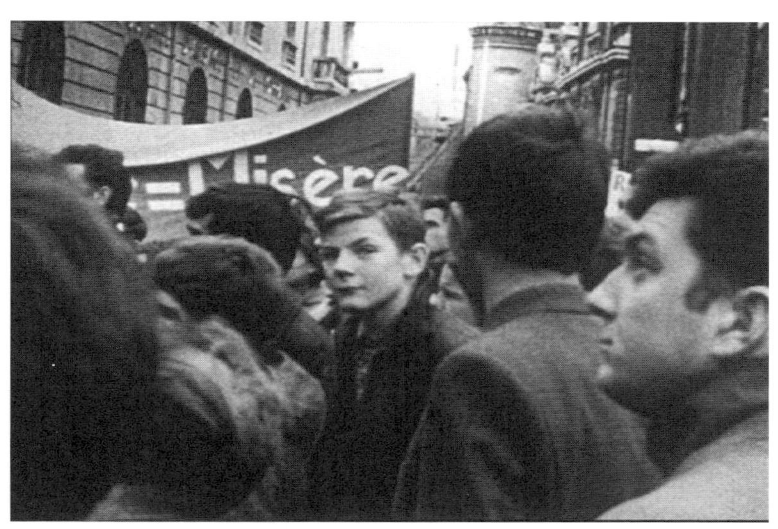

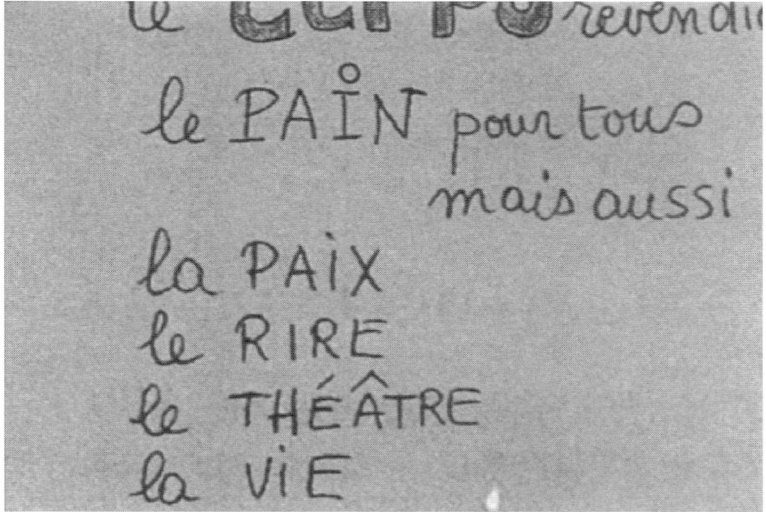

I
Still from Chris
Marker & Mario
Marret, *À bientôt,
j'espère* (1968)

II
Still from Chris
Marker & Mario
Marret, *À bientôt,
j'espère* (1968)

when Yoyo answers Marker's question about how he felt when, for the first time, he climbed onto a barrel and spoke out to the other workers. But this documentary apparatus, which relies on the figure of the filmmaker as author, is disrupted throughout the movie by another tendency that gives control, in a figurative sense, of the camera and the technical features to the workers themselves. In these moments, the filmmaker seems to become immanent to the filmed reality, and a discussion between him, the technicians and the workers begins, replacing the interview and blurring the boundaries between those who represent and the represented: the camera is no longer perceived as a technical medium that produces a binary division, and has become instead an interlocutor. In the same way, the use of the voice-over as a necessarily "transcendent" apparatus is diverted from the classical setting when Marker's voice is replaced by the workers' and activists' own voices, commenting on and explaining their own images. For example, when Yoyo comments on the images of the struggle and explains its organization, the integration of the workers in the support committees, in the functioning of the library, in the cultural events and ends up raising the question of culture as a "political question." This is summarized by a banner that presents the demands of the CCPPO: "bread for everybody, as well as freedom, laughter, theatre, life." And it also happens in the final manifesto when Pol Cèbe states that the right to culture is a political demand in exactly the same manner as the right to bread or the right to housing, even if the employers are less afraid to spell out the word "culture" than they are the words "politics" or "worker's union."[20]

La Charnière

What Pol Cèbe suggests without saying in the film and which is part of the subtext is that the employers' disregard for culture constitutes a breach in the logic of domination, since culture, in this new definition proposed by the CCPPO, fundamentally relates to the distribution of places and roles in the common: by demanding the right to culture, the worker claims a political right, a right to occupy a position that "naturally" does not belong to him, the right to spend his time without working, with something that is in no way connected to work or to the reproduction of his labor force. This is the strategy Rancière has analyzed in his writings on the workers' emancipation movement and more specifically on Gabriel

Gauny, the plebeian philosopher who does not write manifestos or tracts but an apparently apolitical diary in the third person published among reports and statements on the situation in a worker's revolutionary newspaper called *Le Tocsin des travailleurs* [*The Workers' Tocsin*] issued during the French Revolution of 1848.[21] For Rancière, it is "no coincidence that this apparently a-political description was published in a workers' revolutionary newspaper: the possibility of a 'voice of the workers' went through the disqualification of a certain worker's body. It went through the redistribution of the whole set of relationships between capacities and incapacities that define the 'ethos' of a social body. This is also why the same joiner recommends to his friends specific readings: not novels engaging in social issues, but the stories of those romantic characters—Werther, René or Oberman—who suffered from *the misfortune that is forbidden by definition to the worker: the misfortune of having no occupation, of not being fit or equipped for any specific place in society*. What literature does is not providing messages or representations that would give to the workers the awareness of their condition. It is triggering new passions, which means new forms of balance—or imbalance—between an occupation and the sensory equipment fitting it."[22]

The foreshadowing of this imbalance also marks Marker's *À bientôt, j'espère*, since it is inhabited by a fundamental oscillation between a classical use of documentary techniques and the need to break with the hierarchies inscribed in these techniques. This translates into an oscillation between the will to produce knowledge and distribute information about the struggle ("to provide a message") of the working class in Besançon and the will not to adopt a transcendent position in relation to the events. Even though Marker adopts a Foucauldian approach and tries to lead a "struggle side-by-side with those who are fighting and not off to the side trying to enlighten them,"[23] an ambiguity between the filmmaker and those who are filmed lingers that Marker cannot avoid and that becomes very explicit in the last sequence of the film, when Yoyo comes back to the question of culture that he addresses under two aspects: the traditional political or even pragmatic problem of the access to media as a form of mass communication and the media's politics of misinformation regarding the working class. But also and more importantly the need for self-representation of the workers as part of the working class constituted through its struggle, its solidarity and its community. This self-representation is not only articulated through the actual strikes, but also through a new politics of description, which is a self-description of the workers: Yoyo, for instance, describes, with a hesitating smile, the solidarity of the working class as a "culture" that constitutes their power and will result in their victory in the social struggle against inequality and exploitation. There is thus a deferral of the meaning of the word "culture" that gives way to an appropriation by the workers of the words and images that narrate their own story: it is not in order to transmit a better and more authentic message about their struggle, but in order to produce new forms of imbalance in the dominant distribution of the sensible.

This redefinition of culture as the actualization of this imbalance (or of "new passions") is pushed further in the shift between the two films, and it seems that it is incompatible with the oscillation on Marker's side mentioned above and that is addressed by the workers themselves during the first screening of *À bientôt j'espère* in the factory, during which the film and the filmmaker were fiercely criticized by the workers, who felt exploited and objectified. Out of this critique there emerged, recorded as an audio document ironically entitled *La Charnière* [the hinge or the hinge-joint], the idea of the workers of the Rhodiacéta not only participating in the films but creating and showing their own images in order to propose an exercise in dis-identification that could not be so easily reduced to an objectification. They therefore founded the Medvedkin Group in Besançon, and made their first film: *Classe de lutte*.

Classe de lutte

Classe de lutte refers to a twofold claim: in its ambiguity it refers at once to class struggle (*lutte de classes*), and maybe predominantly so, features the pedagogical aspect of the class as a lesson: the film is a lesson in struggle. This lesson is focused primarily on two aspects: to establish the "right to culture" as a political right and to occupy the means of the production of images and discourses. As I have already mentioned, the theoretical and practical demand for a "right to culture" transposes the Rancièrian argument from the scene of writing to the scene of filmmaking, since this right is not to be understood as an access to democratic mass information or entertainment—an ascension to the realm of democratic consensus—but as a *political* right in the Rancièrian sense: it is a political right insofar as its actualization implies a dissolution of the traditional distribution of the social occupations and places. It destabilizes the distribution of the hierarchies between the creative and the non-creative, between the

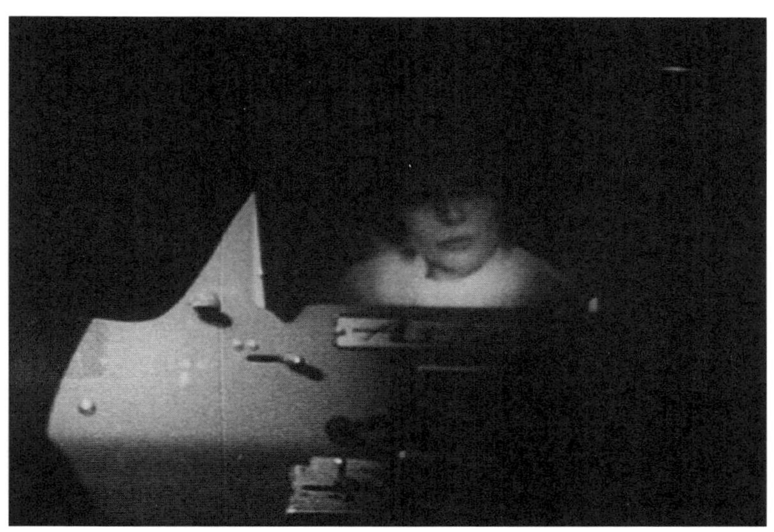

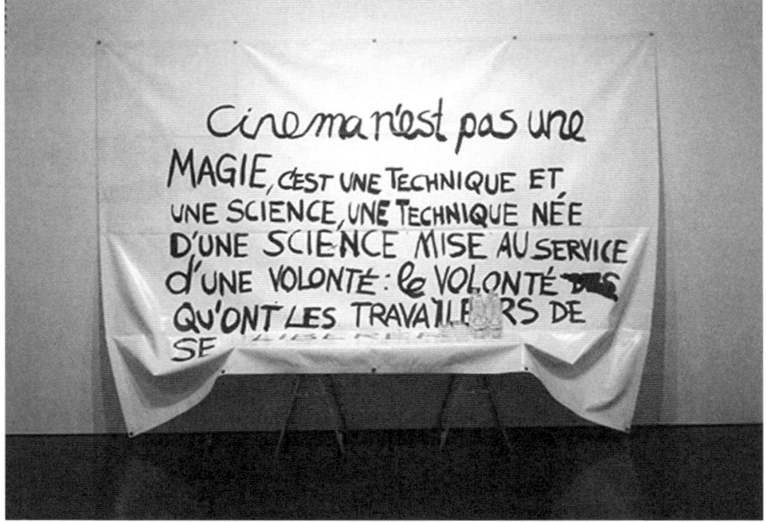

III
Film still from
Groupe Medvedkine
de Besançon, *Classe
de lutte* (1969)

IV
Asier Mendizabal,
*Cinema.*1999 PVC
sheeting, board on
trestles, bottles of
mineral water and
glasses, Courtesy
of Museu d'Art
Contemporani de
Barcelona. Photo:
Seber Ugarte

active and the passive.[24] The first sequence of the film thus presents us with a young woman, Suzanne Zedet, a worker in the Yéma watch-making factory as the central character of this political filmic *Bildungsroman*. Suzanne already appeared in *À bientôt, j'espère*, but only now has come to emancipate herself both as a militant activist and as a woman: while in the 1967 film her husband was literally speaking for her, she has now become an active participant within the social movements at the factory.

The sequence consists of a collage of images that mix private and public scenes and spaces, factory and family life, thereby suggesting the difficulty and even impossibility of separating the two realms.[25] But beyond this exposition of private life as part of the political struggle, the first sequence already thematizes the regime of the image itself through the exhibition of images of the production and distribution of images: the technical support, *i.e.* the camera, the cutting tables or the lighting, that has gone from the hands of the militant filmmakers to the hands of the filmmaking workers has become the subject-matter of the film and establishes its self-reflexive loop. Also, a banner on the wall of the film studio announces: "Cinéma n'est pas une magie, c'est une technique et une science, une technique née d'une science mise au service d'une volonté: la volonté qu'ont les travailleurs de se libérer."[26]

Classe de lutte is therefore a reflection on film as a medium, which is no longer understood as a tool for representation (not even documentary representation), but as an instrument that promotes the struggle of the workers. This is so, because the appropriation of image production machinery by those normally limited to other machines renders unstable the effective partitions and distributions in which the workers work and filmmakers make films as well as those that reserve fictional film to the narration of stories and documentary to the explanation of socially relevant situations. It is precisely in this sense that the shift from *A bientôt, j'espère* to *Classe de lutte* is also led by a change in the filmic language, which no longer uses traditional documentary features such as the interview or the voice-over and tends to use fictionalizing strategies, narrating Suzanne's "personal" story of the worker's movement. By doing so, *Classe de lutte* develops what was already present though not fully accomplished in Marker's arrangement of images, which is still subjected to a logic of explanation that necessarily produces a discourse "about" the working class. On the contrary, for the Medvedkin Group the film constitutes an instrument of *self-description* of the working class by the working class, as an instrument of the narration and constitution of *their* culture through the production of their own counter-discourses and counter-images.

This argument is taken up again at the very end of the film in a less striking but no less effective manner: Suzanne, whose story we have been told, abandons her identity as a working woman, and gives detailed and erudite statements about Picasso and modern art, i.e. she dis-identifies with her role as a militant worker that the film has presented until then, and adopts the role of the art critic, which should "naturally"—i.e. in her natural role as a woman and a worker—not be accessible to her. The dialogue evolves from the paternalism of the factory owners who try to bring an end to the workers' struggle to Picasso and the role that culture, poems and paintings play in the life of the workers: Suzanne deconstructs the conditions that reserve painting and poetry to the bourgeoisie by stating that cultural demands have the same status as the demands concerning salaries and working conditions, and that a poem by Paul Eluard has the same importance as a political discourse.[27]

The film is thus neither a commentary on the workers' struggles or their emancipation nor an explanation of its inner mechanisms or an exercise of contextualization. It does not follow an explanatory logic, but strings together self-reflexive images on the production of images and images that describe Suzanne's life as a militant working woman as well as an art critic. Thus this new construction of Suzanne's identity is itself destabilized both in form and content: through the fictional dimension that is reflected throughout the movements of the camera, the images, the music and the presentation of Suzanne as the main character of her own story; and through Suzanne's dis-identifying move, switching from the working woman to the militant worker and from there to the art critic, so that the dis-identifying gesture of the workers, who take the filming into their own hands, is reflected in the film itself. Therefore, *Classe de lutte* is not only to be understood as the result of workers' will to speak for themselves (*prendre la parole*), but also and perhaps more importantly it marks their determination to produce a work of art, of cinematographic art, a film beyond the boundaries of documentary and fiction, a description beyond explanation. Or as Rancière puts it in his short text on "the historic cultural compromise": the workers—in opposition to some painters, vainly enlisted by the Gauche Prolétarienne in 1972 and 1973—did manage to "inscribe their struggle into the image" and therefore were able to find "a positive politics of the image" within fiction.[28]

As I have shown, the forms of aesthetic realism do not follow the boundaries between different mediums, and can be identified throughout literature, painting, and film. Nevertheless, it is film that re-accentuates the question of a political representation of reality in a specific manner, since it is film (or photography), as a series of mechanically generated images, that claims to be a privileged access to reality, and thus a privileged point of encounter for the political and the aesthetical. *Classe de Lutte* was made in 1968 and produced by the production company SLON (Société pour le Lancement des Œuvres Nouvelles), founded by Chris Marker—a filmmaking collective devoted to making socially and politically conscious works. The film is fully inscribed in the discussions about the political function of cinema, raised on the one hand by the *cinéma vérité*, inaugurated by Edgar Morin and Jean Rouch in their *Chroniques d'un été* (1961) and continued by Marker himself and his *Le joli Mai* (1963), directly inspired by Morin and Rouch.[29] On the other hand, the Medvedkin Groups explicitly establish the connection to Alexander Medvedkin's pedagogically-oriented cinematic production, as in the case of the cine-trains or his propaganda pieces for the Red Army, in which he works, as Dziga Vertov had done before him, with superimpositions and technically modified images. In his propaganda piece *Watch Your Health*, for instance, Medvedkin makes the soldiers who had died from poor hygiene and diseases disappear from the image, with the goal of educating the Red Army soldiers and making them aware of the dangers of the lack of a regular personal hygiene.

If we consider *Classe de Lutte* within this genealogy of Soviet and French political cinema, i.e. within a genealogy of the privileged encounter of the aesthetic with the political and vice versa, it may seem that if we reduce the film to the account, or the quasi-fictional story, of Suzanne's political emancipation (which stands for the political transformation of the working women in general) in a Rancièrian mode, something crucial might get lost—for instance the question of the image as such. Because the film is also a theatrical and/or experimental setting in a Brechtian sense: a setting where the production of images is exhibited as well as the strategies for their appropriation, and where the effects of both the production and its appropriation are experimentally tested.

This is what the work *Cinema* (1999) by the artist Asier Mendizabal is referring to: in his installation, Mendizabal reproduces

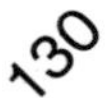

the banner that claims, in an Althusserian manner, cinema to be a science. In his text "Mass and the ideology of form in Asier Mendizabal's practice," Peio Aguirre describes the piece as follows: "The text, written on a white plastic sheet, falls on top of an improvised table supported on simple trestles. On the table, bottles of mineral water and glasses. A cut-out fragment, the text becomes image. Backdrop, too. The scene it projects is that of the excitement of the assembly; long nights without sleep at the service of a mobilized workers organization in the midst of the class struggle and the importance of culture. [...] The staged scene of political representation is converted into the actual representational mechanism that shapes it: the stage set of a possible scene in which militancy, education and didacticism fuse with the cinematic medium at the service of the working class."[30] The work exhibits the movement of appropriation of the symbols of the political moment by producing a theatrical apparatus that suggests the process of production of the banner, the revolution in the process of taking place. The text on the banner thus becomes an image of the strike, in the same way the images of Che and Fidel, or the militant posters for the resistance in Spain and against the war in Vietnam that *Classe de Lutte* presents us as part of the global representation of the European left. *Cinema* re-enacts the conditions of this process of image production, and thereby exposes it as a specific political strategy actualized in a specific moment, and the genealogy of which can be traced back to the two so-called revolutionary moments in European history—1917 and 1968—when cinema and politics met.

Cinema is a specific politics of the image translated into an image and exhibited as an image within the museum's space: it does not engage directly with the literality of the message, but rather establishes a meta-level from which to examine the strategies of auto-representation of the cultural left in the 1960s.[31] The work undertakes an analysis of the discourses, images, documents of this specific nod or encounter of aesthetics and politics, cinema and militancy, and it does so from a "materialistic" perspective, i.e. in order to show that "it isn't the politics that creates its iconography (or its aesthetics), but that the former is the outcome of the *mise en scène* of the latter."[32] *Cinema* introduces the politics of images established in *Classe de Lutte* into an archival paradigm, and therefore functions as a re-contextualization of this aesthetic form of realism, which does not aim at being a "better" representation of a socially relevant reality, but rather at constituting a new political stage understood as the realization of the collapse of a normative distribution of the roles and places within the sensible in which intellectuals know about art, workers know about watchmaking and artists know about filmmaking.

Classe de Lutte, at a specific historical moment, has constituted this stage where such political potentiality is to be enacted: a Rancièrian potentiality of anyone and everyone that correlates to the general availability of subject matter—of the anonymous—to representation. It is this potentiality that is at stake in the post-representative forms of aesthetic realism, the possibility of being something else and thereby abolishing the "natural order," not by merely constructing new identities, but by showing the "constructed character" or artificiality of these very identities. While *Classe de Lutte* performs the former, *Cinema* accentuates the latter. The challenge of the notion of aesthetic realism is therefore that it points to both: the problematization of an identitarian reality producing adequate images of itself and of an objective image pointing to the "natural" identity of its reference. The understanding of the political as a dis-identification gives way to a new politics of the image that is always linked, or is in itself already, an archival practice, i.e. the consideration of an image as part of a specific and always limited archive. This is to say that reality and images are always negotiated and configured anew (but not necessarily in the same way, nor correspondingly) in the struggle between different strategies of distribution of roles and spaces, or of different partitions of the sensible.

1 Jacques Rancière, *The Politics of Aesthetics: The Distribution of the Sensible*, trans. and ed. Gabriel Rockhill (London: Continuum 2004), 24.

2 Walter Benjamin, "Little History of Photography," in *Selected Writings, 1931-1934, vol. II.2* (Boston: Harvard University Press 2005), 527.

3 Here lies the fundamental discord between Realism and Romanticism: even though they share the rejection of classical modes of representation following a normative aesthetics, Romanticism deduces from this rejection a "distance from reality" that creates fantastic and imaginary counter-worlds through the poetization and transfiguration of reality.

4 Jules Champfleury, Letter to Mme Sand, September 1855, reprinted in Linda Nochlin, *Realism and Tradition in Art, 1848-1900. Sources & Documents* (Englewood Cliffs, NJ: Prentice Hall, 1966), 42.

5 Flaubert writes: "La Bovary a été pour moi une affaire de parti pris, un thème." See Gustave Flaubert, Letter to Mme Roger des Genettes October or November 1856 (http://flaubert.univ-rouen.fr/correspondance/conard/outils/1856.htm, last accessed on August 11th, 2011) and his letter to Louise Colet on July 12th 1853: "La vulgarité de mon sujet me donne parfois des nausées, et la difficulté de bien écrire tant de choses si communes encore en perspective m'épouvante. Je suis maintenant achoppé à une scène des plus simples : une saignée et un évanouissement. Cela est fort difficile ; et ce qu'il y a de désolant, c'est de penser que, même réussi dans la perfection, cela ne peut être que passable et ne sera jamais beau, à cause du fond même. Je fais un ouvrage de clown […]" (http://flaubert.univ-rouen.fr/correspondance/conard/outils/1853.htm, last accessed on August 11, 2011).

6 Erich Auerbach, *Mimesis. The Representation of Reality in Western Literature* (Princeton: Princeton University Press, 2003), 487.

7 Erich Auerbach, *Mimesis*, 491. Following Auerbach, Svetlana Alpers has analyzed these phenomena of dis-enclosure in 17th century painting, by transposing Auerbach's statement that the representation of everyday reality in the classical age is only possible through distancing

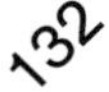

conventions, such as humor, satire, or emphasis. Alpers establishes an analogy between this rule of the separation of styles and the rule of the *ut pictura poesis* painting is subjected to until the Renaissance and that states that the painting is due to illustrate the ahistorical or mythological action or event. Alpers shows how the rupture with this rule is performed by Velázquez in his *Hilanderas*, when he highlights the everyday life of the working women by moving it to the foreground of the painting, banning the mythological scene to the background. The painting thus realizes the dissolution of the primacy of action over description and undergoes the central norm of classical representation. Hegel insists in his *Vorlesungen zur Ästhetik* on a similar point when he states that the depicted details are themselves the metonymy of political reality: as for example the obsession for details of Dutch genre painting or the depiction of the light-heartedness and carefreeness of Murillo's young beggars that point to a new regime of representation in which these insignificant details mark at once the liberty and vividness of the representation and point to the newly won freedom and liberation of the Dutch people from the Spanish rule. See Svetlana Alpers, "Describe or Narrate? A Problem in Realistic Representation," *New Literary History*, Vol. 8, No. 1 (Autumn 1976), 15-41; G.W.F. Hegel, *Vorlesungen zur Ästhetik*, "Das Verhältnis des Ideals zur Natur," in *Werke* 13 (Frankfurt/Main, 2007); see also Jacques Rancière, "Politik des Ästhetischen," (manuscript), Cologne, May 13, 2009.

8 Walter Benjamin, "Little Story of Photography," 510.

9 Ibid.

10 Cf. Hito Steyerl, "Die dokumentarische Unschärferelation. Was ist Dokumentarismus?," in *Die Farbe der Wahrheit. Dokumentarismen im Kunstfeld* (Vienna: Turia und Kant, 2008), 7-16.

11 Jacques Rancière, "Are some things representable?," in *The Future of the Image* (London: Verso 2007), 118.

12 Jacques Rancière, *Disagreement*, trans. Jacqueline Rose (Minneapolis: University of Minnesota Press), 36.

13 Ibid., 40.

14 Michel Foucault, "Lives of Infamous Men", in *Power. Essential Works of Foucault, 1954-1984: Volume Three* (New York, 2002) 157-75; 161.

15 Ibid., 173.

16 Ibid.

17 bid.,174.

18 Chris Marker and Mario Marret, *A bientôt, j'espère*, France 1986, 3'38-6'20.

19 Bill Nichols speaks in this context of a "Voice-of-God commentary" that characterizes the *expository documentary*. This moralizing trait will then disappear in the observational documentary that seems to adopt—thanks to mobile and unremarkable cameras and technical equipment—a neutral observer position. Both are opposed to the interactive and reflexive documentary whose aim is "to make the conventions of representation themselves more apparent and to challenge the impression of reality which the other three modes normally conveyed unproblematically." Bill Nichols, *Representing Reality* (Indianapolis: Indiana University Press, 1991), 33.

20 Chris Marker and Mario Marret, *A bientôt j'espère*, 3'38-6'20.

21 "Believing himself at home, he loves the arrangement of a room, so long as he has not finished laying the floor. If the window opens out onto a garden or commands a view of picturesque horizon, he stops his arms and glides in imagination toward the spacious view to enjoy it better than the possessors of the neighbouring residences." Gabriel Gauny, "Le travail à la tâche," *Le Tocsin des Travailleurs* (June 1848), in Gabriel Gauny, *Le Philosophe plébéien, textes choisis et présentés par Jacques Rancière* (Paris: La Découverte/ Presses Universitaires de Vincennes, 1983), 91. As cited in Jacques Rancière, *The Nights of Labor*, trans. John Drury (Philadelphia: Temple University Press, 1989), 81.

22 Jacques Rancière, "Aesthetic Separation, Aesthetic Community. Scenes from the Aesthetic Regime of Art," in *Art&Research, A Journal of Ideas, Contexts and Methods*. Volume 2, No. 1 (Summer 2008), http://www.artandresearch.org.uk/v2n1/ranciere.html; my emphasis.

23 Michel Foucault and Gilles Deleuze, "Intellectuals and power," in *Gilles Deleuze, Desert Islands and other texts* (New York: Semiotext[e], 2004), 207.

24 It thus refers back to a right to leisure in the sense of free, non-reproductive time: the right to "waste time" and to be "un-determined," or as Theodor W. Adorno puts it: "Rien faire comme une bête, auf dem Wasser liegen und friedlich in den Himmel schauen, 'sein, sonst nichts, ohne alle weitere Bestimmung und Erfüllung'" ["*Rien faire comme une bête*, lying on water and looking peacefully up at the sky, 'being nothing else, without any further definition and fulfillment.'"]. See Theodor W. Adorno, "Sur l'eau" in Theodor W. Adorno, *Minima Moralia. Reflexionen aus dem beschädigten Leben* (Suhrkamp, 1969), 208; *Minima Moralia*, trans. E.F.N. Jephcott (London: NLB, 1974), 157.

25 Groupe Medvedkine de Besançon, *Classe de lutte*, France 1969, 0'10-3'07.

26 "The cinema is not magic, it is a technology and a science, a technology that comes from science and is placed in the service of a will: the will of the workers to liberate themselves."

27 *Casse de lutte*, 34'17-36'40.

28 Jacques Rancière, "Le compromis culturel historique" (1978), in *Les scènes du peuple* (Lyon, 2003), 262.

29 In her work *After Before* (2005), Sharon Hayes repeats this man/woman-on-the streets-interviews in New York City in the months of September and October 2004, and recently Sarah Pierce has invited students in art, sociology and politics to a screening of *Chronique d'un été* in Bilbao, Spain

133

and Copenhagen, Denmark among other places, followed each time by a roundtable discussion about the very questions raised by Morin and Rouch that are documented in her ongoing film project. The question would be the answer to the question, "Are you happy?"

30 Peio Aguirre, "Mass and the ideology of form in Asier Mendizabal's practice," in Asier Mendizabal, *Disjecta membra* (Barcelona: MACBA, 2008), 45.

31 This seems to be a general strategy in Mendizabal's work that establishes a fragmentary archive of the militant image production of the European 1960s that the artist appropriates through a process of recopying, reprinting or redrawing as in the case of the banner from *Classe de Lutte*, or, as in *No Time for Love* (2000), the manual reproduction of the film poster of Costa-Gavras's *Z* from 1969, another symbol of political film. Aguirre suggests that Mendizabal's work departs from the conviction (as does Jean-Luc Godard) that politics is unrepresentable in the same way as reality itself. It is therefore only through this exact or mechanical reproduction of the symbolic images that the reference—reality—enters the field of discourse: the symbol, the image does not refer to anything beyond itself but only exists as such, as an image in an archive of images.

32 Peio Aguirre, "Mass and the ideology of form in Asier Mendizabal's practice," 46.

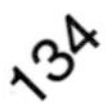

9

I HAVE A DREAM

Annette Weisser

While preparing to write this text I had a dream. A didactic constellation: one female teacher, one male teacher, and two schoolgirls. With some urgency I ask the two teachers the following question: "But what is the opposite of language?" The woman answers "performance," the man replies "text." I turn to my fellow pupil, whose German is not so strong, in order to explain their words. But my Japanese friend just smiles and presents me with a drawing she dashed off during the brief exchange. It demonstrates that she very well understood what has been said. For my part, I realize her drawing offers me a third possible answer to my question, and that my friend is now my teacher.

I see this dream as being linked in diverse ways to the basic theme of the conference "Everything is in Everything: From Aesthetic Education to Intellectual Emancipation," which I co-organized with my colleague Jason Smith in March 2011. How does the theory of art relate, in broad terms, to the practice of art? In an academic environment, how permeable, or reversible, are the power structures and the gender assignments? In what way are these structures and assignments subject to constant reproduction in language, and what would amount to the "opposite" of this language?

Let's switch to the classroom. Together with two tutors a small group of art students are working through a selection of texts by Jacques Rancière. This endeavor might be summed up as laborious groping marked by frustration and occasional boredom relieved by intermittent flashes of excitement and understanding, which are amplified by the act of sharing. Philosophy as a primal experience: as the social experience of reciprocal mindfulness, but also as an almost physical sensation of reluctance, the feeling of being an inadequate beginner in a place that by definition promises professionalization and intellectual sovereignty. The purported luxury of having two tutors at once turns out to be a necessary one because the posing of seemingly dumb questions has to be practiced as well. Among the texts that are being read together is Rancière's *The Ignorant Schoolmaster*, a highly complex illustration, and at the same time rupturing, of the classroom situation.

Why do artists subject themselves to this occasionally masochistic process? One common rejoinder is that the production of art, which is perceived as problematic because of its commodity character, undergoes "sublimation" in the course of the artmakers' intellectual endeavors. A rarely questioned art school dogma decrees that tackling philosophy and, more generally, theoretical texts makes artistic output more complex and interesting, thus enhances the quality of the product. (Another art school dogma, still prevalent at many German art academies, decrees of course exactly the opposite.) But as the analysis undertaken in recent years of "cognitive capitalism" has thoroughly demonstrated, knowledge and thinking are subject to the same market mechanisms as art objects and their production. (This is reflected by, among other things, the countless new Ph.D. programs for artists.) In my view, this actual process of sublimation receives too little attention. Teachers rely rather on theoretical meteorites striking with such impact that, somehow or another, the students' production will be propelled on the right orbit. Sticking with the metaphor, it is not necessarily the case that the material from the neighboring galaxy organically bonds with the existing structures of thought. And if no such bonding occurs, the theory just lies dormant, a foreign body in people's minds, or a hardcover fetish that lies about, unread, in artists' studios.

So how can creative, even subversive, energy be derived from this impact? One suggestion: by affirmatively occupying the gap between theory and artistic practice, by moving away from the academicisms of either field and towards confident and self-reflexive dilettantism. This minimal shift in valuations can be directly experienced as empowerment: just as a hybrid engine wins energy when accelerating and braking alike, so it is a question of making the inner reluctance felt when working through arduous texts part of the way the text is understood. This experience of reluctance, of being overwhelmed, amounts to negative intellectual energy, and as such it is a resource that can be put to productive use. If such a shift is negotiated successfully, authority is withdrawn from the text and restored to one's own mind, and intellectual emancipation occurs.

One might justifiably query whether the academy, of all places, is the right place to practice dilettantism. But for the sake of argument let us assume the current situation to be one in which the academies, having long lost their monopoly over the production of knowledge, are seeking to regain command by expanding the copyright, patenting, global standardization and certification of knowledge, research, and the like. An institution that sees itself as progressive might respond to such a situation by renouncing precisely this function of control, and instead position itself as a node within a network of public schools, reading groups, biohackers and similar non-aligned temporary associations. Such an institution would not do so in a way that craves acceptance and strives for street credibility, but would make resources available and offer equal partners the possibility of exchange. By necessity, it would be a matter of rescinding the dichotomy of inside and outside within the institutional power structure, and of viewing dilettantism and professionalism as two poles within a continuous and fluid process. The day-to-day reality of most creative workers is characterized by such fluidity. The experience of how differently one and the same text "performs" depending on whether it is read inside or outside an institutional context would fall by the wayside, but there are more and more signs that the idea of "outside" is a romantic notion from the twentieth century, and whether one attends an academy or the public school in order to meet the demands of cognitive capitalism or to learn how to put up resistance to the latter, it comes down to much the same thing in the end.

(Note to self: Organize conference on dilettantism)

But what would a potential form for this affirmative occupation of the gap between two (or more) disciplines be? With the benefit of hindsight I would say we gave too little consideration to this question while preparing the conference. Hardly surprisingly, the choice of the conference format privileges exclusive academic discourse, and for that reason a certain ability to hold one's own in such an environment was among the criteria for selecting the artist speakers. In the wider conference setting it proved impossible to reproduce something achieved, over and over again, in the smaller groups, namely the collective attempts to grasp the concepts, the links forged between the theoretical reading matter and personal experience. The vast majority of the audience of art students and artists stayed silent. This silence was all the more grave because the conference was aimed at intellectual emancipation. The exploration of new formats in which the three communication modes of text, performance and drawing are placed as equals alongside each other, and every participant is at once teacher and pupil, actor and observer—that is, as becomes clear to me while writing, the stuff of my dream. The Graduate Studies in Art program at Art Center, with its strong focus on philosophy, would be an ideal place for future experiments. I think, for instance, of the structure of an international soccer tournament: beginning with sixteen work groups, the main theses emerge in the course of two weeks and play against each other in the grand finale. In order to avoid unnecessary bloodshed, the rulebook would best be borrowed from the UNO.

Let us return to the classroom. "Equality" is on today's agenda. Based on Joseph Jacotot's axiom of the equality of intelligences, Jacques Rancière develops the inconceivable idea that "equality" already exists. Not as a distant promise, as the reward to be redeemed at the end of a war successfully waged against global capitalism, but as a hypothesis requiring constant actualization. The sporadic rejection practiced on the micro-level of modes of behavior aimed at dominance and exploitation makes it possible to experience, situationally, in the here-and-now, the remote goal of social equality, and this experience, having actually taken place, functions as an agent of social change. So let's actualize, say the clever students: With professors' salaries including medical insurance, it's easy enough for you to talk about revolution. Whereas we pay a lot of money to gain access to a system you constantly discredit, although you participate in it just like all those who simply sell their art in galleries and are content to do so. And, clever students, you're absolutely right.

NOTES ON CONTRIBUTORS

Arne De Boever teaches American Studies in the School of Critical Studies at the California Institute of the Arts. He also directs the School's MA Program in Aesthetics and Politics. He has published numerous articles on literature, film, and critical theory and is editor of *Parrhesia: A Journal of Critical Philosophy*. His book *States of Exception in the Contemporary Novel* will be published by Continuum.

Claire Fontaine is a Paris-based collective artist, founded in 2004. After lifting her name from a popular brand of school notebooks, Claire Fontaine declared herself a "readymade artist" and began to elaborate a version of neo-conceptual art that often looks like other people's work. Working in neon, video, sculpture, painting and text, her practice can be described as an ongoing interrogation of the political impotence and the crisis of singularity that seem to define contemporary art today. Recent exhibitions include "After Marx April, After Mao June," Aspen Art Museum, Colorado; "Future Tense," El Museo Tamayo Arte Contemporáneo, Mexico D.F.; "Economies," Museum of Contemporary Art, North Miami; "Closed for Prayers," Dvir Gallery, Hangar 2, Jaffa Port, Israel; "Etrangers Partout (QDM)," Nuit Blanche, Belleville, Paris; "Kultur ist ein Palast der aus Hundescheiße gebaut ist.," MD72, Berlin; "Arando en el mar/Ploughing the sea," Gaga Arte Contemporaneo, Mexico D.F.; "Fighting Gravity," Regina Gallery London and Moscow. Claire Fontaine also participated in the May 18, 2006 colloquium, "Esthétique et politique, autour de la philosophie de Jacques Rancière," held in Stockholm and which featured Alexandre Costanzo and Jacques Rancière.

Peter Friedl is an artist based in Berlin. His artistic practice emphasizes the friction between aesthetic and political awareness, employing strategies such as permanent displacement, editing, or over-exposing. Recent solo exhibitions include "Magnificence," Guido Costa Projects, Turin (2011); Sala Rekalde, Bilbao (2010);

"Blow Job," Extra City Kunsthal Antwerpen (2008); "Working," Kunsthalle Basel (2008); "OUT OF THE SHADOWS," Witte de With, Center for Contemporary Art, Rotterdam (2004). In 2006, the Museu d'Art Contemporani de Barcelona (MACBA) organized a comprehensive retrospective survey, "Peter Friedl: Work 1964–2006," which was subsequently shown at Miami Art Central/Miami Art Museum (2007) and the Musée d'Art Contemporain in Marseille (2007). Friedl's work has been exhibited worldwide, including at documenta X (1997) and documenta 12, Kassel (2007), the 48th Venice Biennale (1999), the 3rd Berlin Biennale (2004), the 2nd International Biennial of Contemporary Art in Seville (2006), Manifesta 7, Trento (2008), the 7th Gwangju Biennale (2008), the 28th Bienal de São Paulo (2008), and Tirana International Contemporary Art Biennial (2009). Since the 1980s, Friedl has published numerous essays and book projects such as *Four or Five Roses* (2004), *Working at Copan* (2007), and *Playgrounds* (2008). *Secret Modernity: Selected Writings and Interviews 1981–2009* (Sternberg Press) was published in 2010.

Jeremy Gilbert-Rolfe is Chair of Graduate Studies in Art at Art Center and also a Visiting Tutor at the Royal Academy Schools in London. His most recent one-person exhibition was at Alexander Gray Associates, New York (2011) and his most recent book was *Beauty and the Contemporary Sublime* (2000). His next exhibition will be as part of the collaborative Awkward × 2, which he and Rebecca Norton formed in the summer of 2010, at The Suburban, Chicago, in October 2011. *Jeremy Gilbert-Rolfe: Art after Deconstruction*, edited by Rex Butler (2011) will contain two new essays by him as well as essays about his work by four other writers. He was awarded NEA Fellowships in Criticism (1974) and in Painting (1979 and 1989), the CAA's Frank Jewett Mather Award for Art or Architectural Criticism in 1998, a Guggenheim Fellowship for Painting in 1997 and a Francis Greenberger Award for Lifetime Achievement in the Arts in 2001.

Maria Muhle studied philosophy and political science in Madrid and Paris. Since 2008, she has been Academic Assistant to the Chair for History and Theory of Artificial Worlds, Institute for Media Studies, Bauhaus-Universität Weimar and held the Junior Professorship for Philosophy of Media and Techniques at the Institute for Media Studies at Ruhr-Universität Bochum in 2010. Her research focuses on contemporary political and aesthetic theory, and especially on the notion of "aesthetic realism" in the context of a political aesthetics. She is also the co-founder of August Verlag Berlin, a publishing house for theory at the crossroads of philosophy, politics and arts and works as a freelance art critic. Recent publications include "Biopolitics and life. Foucault and Canguilhem," in *The Government of Life*, ed. Vanessa Lemm and Miguel Vatter (New York: Fordham Univ. Press, forthcoming); "Zweierlei Vitalismus," in *Gilles Deleuze: Philosophie und Nicht-Philosophie*, ed. Friedrich Balke and Mark Rölli (2011); and "Political art as aesthetic realism or passion of the real?," *Texte zur Kunst*, n° 80 (2010).

Jacques Rancière is Emeritus Professor at the University of Paris-VIII, where he taught Philosophy from 1969 to 2000.

Frank Ruda holds a research position at the Collaborative Research Centre 626 at the Freie Universität Berlin. He is co-editor of the book series "morale provisoire" at the Berlin-based publishing house Merve. He has translated works by Badiou and Rancière into German and has published broadly on questions of contemporary philosophy. His publications include *Hegel's Rabble: An Investigation into Hegel's Philosophy of Right* (Continuum, 2011) and "Humanism Reconsidered, or: Life living Life," in *Filozofski vestnik* (2009).

Jason E. Smith is Assistant Professor in the Graduate Studies in Art Department at Art Center College of Design (Pasadena). He writes on contemporary art, continental philosophy and political theory, and his work has recently appeared in *Artforum*, *Critical Inquiry*, *Critical Companion to Contemporary Marxism*, *Grey Room*, *Parrhesia*, *Texte zur Kunst* and *Theory & Event*, among other places. With Philip Armstrong, he recently published a long interview with Jean-Luc Nancy, *Politique et au-delà* (Galilée, 2011). He is currently writing a book on the films of Guy Debord.

Jan Voelker holds a research position at the Collaborative Research Centre 626 at the Freie Universität Berlin. His research and publications focus on Kantian aesthetics, contemporary political thought and the relation between art and politics. He is co-editor of the series "morale provisoire" at the Berlin-based publisher Merve and has co-translated works of Alain Badiou and Jacques Rancière into German.

Publications include *Ästhetik der Lebendigkeit. Kants dritte Kritik* [Aesthetics of Liveliness, Kant's Third Critique] (2011); *Beyond Potentialities? Politics between the Possible and the Impossible* (diaphanes 2011); *Alain Badiou, Ist Politik denkbar?*, ed. and trans. with Frank Ruda (2010); Jacques Rancière, *Ist Kunst widerständig?*, ed. and trans. with Frank Ruda (2008); and *Alain Badiou, Die kommunistische Hypothese*, ed. and trans. with Frank Ruda (2011).

Annette Weisser is an artist living and working in Los Angeles and Berlin. Since 2007 Assistant Professor at Art Center College of Design, Graduate Fine Art Program. Recent solo shows: "Alle Tage Abstraktion," Galerie Reception, Berlin (2011); "The End of the World," Galerie Reception, Berlin (2010). Recent group shows include "Belvedere," Arp Museum, Remagen (2011); *(re)designing nature*, Künstlerhaus Wien, Vienna travelled to Städtische Galerie, Bremen (2011); *Parkliv*, Marabouparken, Sundbyberg, Sweden (2010); "Heartland," Van Abbe Museum Eindhoven (2008), travelled to SMART Museum, Chicago (2009). Besides her artistic practice, Annette Weisser has published essays and reviews on art, urbanism and cultural activism in magazines such as *Texte zur Kunst, Springerin, SPEX, Afterall,* and *die tageszeitung.* She co-curated the exhibitions "World Watchers," Neue Gesellschaft für Bildende Kunst, Berlin (2004) and "Arbeitshaus," Kunsthaus Dresden (2005). Annette Weisser is a founding member of "Detroit Tree of Heaven Woodshop."

Evan Calder Williams is the author of *Combined and Uneven Apocalypse* (Zero Books, 2011) and *Roman Letters* (Oslo Editions, 2011) and writes regularly for *Film Quarterly* and *Mute.* He currently resides in Naples, where he is a Fulbright Fellow.

Everything is
in Everything:

Jacques Rancière
Between Intellectual
Emancipation and
Aesthetic Education

Jacques Rancière
Jeremy Gilbert-Rolfe
Frank Ruda
Arne de Boever
Peter Friedl
Jan Voelker
Claire Fontaine
Jason E. Smith
Evan Calder Williams
Maria Muhle
Annette Weisser

Edited by
Jason E. Smith &
Annette Weisser

Design
Mark Owens with
Andrew Lister

Printed in China
Oceanic Graphic
Printing, Inc.

© 2011 the authors
and Art Center
Graduate Press

Distributed by

JRP|Ringier
Letzigraben 134
CH-8047 Zurich
T +41 (0) 43 311 27 50
F +41 (0) 43 311 27 51
E info@jrp-ringier.com
www.jrp-ringier.com

ISBN
978-3-03764-265-8

JRP|Ringier publica-
tions are available
internationally at
selected bookstores
and from the following
distribution partners:

Switzerland
AVA
Verlagsauslieferung
AG, Centralweg 16,
CH-8910 Affoltern a.A.,
verlagsservice@ava.ch,
www.ava.ch

Germany and Austria
Vice Versa Vertrieb
Immanuelkirchstrasse
12, D-10405 Berlin,
info@vice-versa-
vertrieb.de, www.
vice-versa-vertrieb.de

France
Les presses du réel
35 rue Colson,
F-21000 Dijon,
info@lespressesdureel.
com, www.lespresses-
dureel.com

UK and other European
Countries
Cornerhouse Publications
70 Oxford Street,
UK-Manchester M1
5NH, publications@
cornerhouse.org, www.
cornerhouse.org/books

USA, Canada, Asia, and
Australia
ARTBOOK | D.A.P.
155 Sixth Avenue, 2nd
Floor, USA-New York,
NY 10013, dap@dapinc.
com, www.artbook.com

For a list of our partner
bookshops or for any
general questions,
please contact
JRP|Ringier directly
at info@jrp-ringier.com,
or visit our homepage
www.jrp-ringier.com
for further information
about our program.